THE MINISTRY OF THE VOLUNTEER TEACHER

The MINISTRY of the VOLUNTEER TEACHER

CHARLES R. FOSTER

ABINGDON PRESS
NASHVILLE

The Ministry of the Volunteer Teacher

Copyright © 1986 by Abingdon Press

Library of Congress Cataloging in Publication Data

FOSTER, CHARLES R., 1937-
  The ministry of the volunteeer teacher.
  Bibliography: p.
  1. Sunday-school teachers. I. Title.
BV1534.F63   1986   268'.1   85-21440
      ISBN 0-687-27040-5 (pbk.: alk. paper)

Scripture quotations noted TEV are from the *Good News Bible*, the Bible in Today's English Version. Copyright ©
American Bible Society 1966, 1971, 1976.

MAUFACTURED BY THE PARTHENON PRESS AT
NASHVILLE, TENNESSEE, UNITED STATES OF AMERICA

To the teachers of the
First United Methodist Church
Corning, New York
1963–66

with whom I first began
this conversation

CONTENTS

A Word to the Reader   **9**

Part I - The Volunteer Teacher Is in Ministry   **11**
  1 The Volunteer Teacher Is Called   **14**
  2 The Volunteer Teacher Is Gifted   **18**

Part II - The Responsibility of the Volunteer Teacher   **21**
  3 The Responsibility to Bind the Generations   **22**
  4 The Responsibility to Build Up the Community of Faith
      to Glorify God and to Serve Neighbor   **24**
  5 The Responsibility to Instruct for Faithful Discipleship
      and Responsible Living   **28**

Part III - The Work of the Volunteer Teacher: To Create
            an Environment of Caring   **33**
  6 The Task of Making God's Care Visible   **34**
  7 The Task of Creating a Caring Community   **46**
  8 The Task of Being a Caregiver   **52**

Part IV - The Work of the Volunteer Teacher: To Mediate Good
            News from Our Past for Our Future   **59**
  9 Students and Teachers: The "Who" in Teaching   **61**
 10 Objectives: The "Why" of Teaching   **65**
 11 Content: The "What" of Teaching   **68**
 12 Method: The "How" of Teaching   **72**
 13 Strategy: The "When and Where" of Teaching   **82**
 14 Evaluation: The "What Happened" While Teaching   **87**
Postscript   **91**
Notes   **93**
For Further Reading on the Ministry of Teaching   **95**

A WORD TO THE READER

Several years ago I started to write a book on the church's ministry with children. I spent several months in research. I developed a general outline and then began writing. The first chapter on attitudes in our society toward children went fairly smoothly. The second chapter proved to be difficult. I threw away several attempts.

One day, however, I realized that my concern for children centered primarily on the gap between our dreams for their future and the reality of their experience in families, churches, schools, and the agencies of our society charged with helping them. This breakthrough was quickly followed by another. I realized that the abdication of the teaching task at so many points in our society contributed to this gap. The book I really wanted to write to reflect my concern for children had to do with teaching. So I set aside the manuscript I had started and began again. The result was *Teaching in the Community of Faith*, published in 1982 by Abingdon Press.

That exercise of writing on the nature of the teaching task in a community of faith made me increasingly aware that teaching has dominated my attention and much of my energy for almost thirty years. It has been at the heart of my own understanding of my calling into ministry. I began to teach in a formal and designated role when I was sixteen in the Sunday school my family attended. I taught junior high groups all the way through seminary. My concern for teaching quickly turned to the training of teachers. This interest prompted me to become certified to teach youth leaders and teachers in my own denomination. I have taught groups of all ages—preschool and elementary age children, teenagers, and adults. I have taught in the church and in seminary and graduate schools. At the same time, I continue to be engaged in the teaching of teachers—both professional and volunteer.

I rehearse this personal history primarily to observe a shift in my focus on the work of teachers. For years I was caught up in the experience of teaching itself. Although I experienced frustration at many points, it was offset by the pleasure I received from planning for a teaching event. It was forgotten when my teaching helped people explore new ideas and develop new skills. Recently my attention has shifted to trying to understand the support structures in the church and society that are important to the work of teachers in general and to volunteer teachers in the church in particular.

I have become increasingly concerned with the way the church often views its volunteer teachers. In many respects teaching is one of the most demanding of all volunteer leadership roles. It requires considerable time, and the task is relentless. As soon as one class session is over, another must be prepared. Students are often resistant or apathetic, and their attendance is often irregular. The teacher's own faith, knowledge, and skills are constantly on the line. Yet the support and overt rewards for teaching are often minimal. Teaching is usually experienced as a lonely job. With the exception of some teachers of adult classes or the leader of a popular program for teenagers, many teachers are unknown to the rest of the congregation or parish. How often I have heard people say, "I didn't know you were teaching," to someone who had been in the classroom for three or more years. This passive lack of support contributes to inadequate training and inspires little or no attention to the volunteer teacher's own spiritual growth.

Perhaps even more serious has been my growing awareness of the ways the role of the teacher is diminished—even demeaned—by the church community. When a recruiter or a pastor says to prospective teachers that it really does not matter if they know enough to teach or that all they have to do is "love the children," he or she is promoting a future for the church built on ignorance and incompetence in matters of faith. When recruiters say teaching will not take much time, they lie if they also expect teaching to be taken seriously. Perhaps the demeaning of the role of the teacher is most evident in the majority of books written for the volunteer teacher. After a brief introduction, which makes clear the author is writing for teachers in the church, the remainder of all too many books concentrates upon technical skills for teaching. While these books are often useful, they do not clarify the relationship of the technical to the religious aspects of teaching.

It is to this latter task that I have addressed this book. It is my hope that you will find it to be a helpful resource. In the pages that follow, I examine the responsibilities and tasks every teacher faces to varying degrees. I explore the relationship of the ministry of the teacher to the work of the church as the body of Christ in the world. Most of all I celebrate the ministry of the volunteer teacher. The apostle Paul stressed the importance of this ministry in his letters to those first churches. We can do no less.

If you are a volunteer teacher in the church or are considering the possibility of becoming one, this book has been written for you. While writing it, I have imagined myself in conversation with some of the volunteer teachers with whom I have worked over the years. Many of the issues first came to my attention during planning meetings or workshop sessions with teachers. They have been refined in conversations with teachers over the past twenty years. I hope you will experience this book as a continuation of those conversations. I would suggest, if at all possible, that you read and discuss it with someone else. You may find the questions and exercises throughout the text helpful in that process. You may wish to use it as a text in a class for teachers in your church or as part of a workshop. However you use or read the book, I hope you find it useful in clarifying your role as a teacher and in helping to improve your teaching.

Before we begin our conversation I would like to recognize those people who have directly influenced me while writing the pages that follow. The ideas for the book began with a conversation with Richard Cookson and Warren Hartman of the Board of Discipleship of The United Methodist Church. The manuscript was refined and edited after I received comments and suggestions from several volunteer teachers, Christian educators, and pastors: Barbara King, Duane Ewers, Mary Jane Pierce Norton, Debbie Pitney, John Pitney, and Roy Ryan. Ongoing conversations with my wife, Janet, my graduate assistant, David Otto (whose research and suggestions especially influenced chapter 12), and the Scarritt Graduate School Christian education faculty secretary, Mary Slater (who also typed the various versions of the manuscript) have helped to clarify many of my thoughts and ideas. To these people and to you, my readers, I am grateful.

CHARLES R. FOSTER

PART I

The Volunteer Teacher Is in Ministry

Introduction

Volunteer teachers are special people. I first learned this fact through my own experience. My life has been graced by faithful and dedicated volunteer teachers. Mrs. Wynn, for example, taught the "junior class" in one Sunday school I attended. I remember the calm authority with which this former deaconess conducted our class and the stern simplicity of her dress and manner. Her class sessions were well-organized, and our behavior was firmly controlled. My memories of her teaching, however, dwell on the fun we had singing and the pleasure we experienced in implementing our research in the Bible in a variety of creative projects. Nothing seemed to be too big a challenge or too messy for Mrs. Wynn—if we did our background work well.

Mrs. Selnes, my junior high teacher in another Sunday school, was quite different. I remember her gentleness and her concern for each of us. She was not a creative teacher. We each took a turn reading a paragraph from the "quarterly" and discussed the "lesson" at the end of the session. The genuine care she showed for us, however, not only on Sunday but throughout the week, "taught" us as effectively as any imaginative class could about the redemptive love of God.

Other names and faces come to mind. Mr. Patton was not intimidated by our adolescent questions. Dorothy Patch challenged the superficiality of our faith and the self-centeredness in our views of justice.

Grandma Handley's adventurous energy and vision at 84 years more than challenged the group of lively teenagers with whom she worked. The impact of these volunteer teachers on my life cannot be overestimated. Neither can the ministry of volunteer teachers in the church down through the ages and around the world.

The ministry of teaching has been considered of primary importance throughout the history of the Christian movement. Jesus first commissioned his disciples to go into the villages "to teach." When describing the gifts central to the task of building up the body of Christ, Paul consistently emphasized the importance of teaching. In all the missionary movements of the church, from the journeys of Paul to the present, teachers have been given a primary role and place. This emphasis on teaching should not surprise us.

To understand this function we must first clarify the way I am using the word *community* in the pages that follow. A community is any group of people who share a common identity and a common history. It binds people together in structures and relationships that provide continuity over time. It is guided by a vision for the future of the community *located* in the meanings of significant events in the past. In this sense, a community can be a family, a congregation, a denomination, as well as a nation. Each has a name. Each has a heritage or history filled with stories of events that have brought its people to this point in time. Each has an organizational structure. Part of it is informal, consisting of attitudes, values, and customs. Each community finds its purpose for being in certain events like the Exodus, the Incarnation, the Declaration of Independence. The meanings of those events help distinguish one community from another. So when we speak of the church as a community of faith, we are emphasizing the commonality of our loyalty to Jesus Christ, our shared Jewish and Christian heritage, and the bond of the structures and organizations which gather us into congregations and parishes.[1]

It is the life and purposes of a given community that give direction to the work of a teacher. The teacher stands self-consciously as a bridge between a community's memory of its past and the vision for its future. Walter Brueggemann has reminded us that the teacher's task helps maintain the life of a community across the generations. The teacher seeks to keep the past alive so that the faith and wisdom of our ancestors are not lost. The teacher also seeks to shape the future so that we do not end up making fossils of the doctrines and institutions we have inherited.[2] The teacher's responsibility is a major one. The vitality of any community, including a given congregation or parish, is dependent in part on the effectiveness of its teachers. No wonder teachers are special people.

Volunteer teachers in the church belong to a special fellowship. It may be traced back to the experience of the disciples meeting together after the resurrection appearances of Jesus before moving out to "teach good news." The fellowship was expanded as some of those taught by the disciples later became teachers and further still, as some of their students also became teachers. Like the ripples that expand from the place we threw a pebble into a pond, each new generation of teachers finds itself both sharing in the experience of those who preceded it and handing on that experience to those who

follow. Jesus began teaching. Then we discover the disciples teaching. Later we read of another generation of teachers that included Mark, Barnabas, and Timothy. Church historians fill in the names that come later: Tertullian, Augustine, Thomas Aquinas, Erasmus, Martin Luther, and so on down to the present. The names of most teachers in the church are lost to us, but we stand in the circles of their influence. We are the products of their efforts.

This fellowship not only gathers up all who have taught through the ages. It extends around the world. In spite of the fact that we often feel quite alone as teachers in our own churches, we actually belong to a vast fellowship. In my own denomination there were more than 428,000 volunteer teachers in 1984. They make up only a small part of the fellowship of volunteer teachers to be found in the various denominations in the United States. And that number is still no more than a small part of the total number of volunteer teachers in the churches around the world.

Some of us teach in Protestant Sunday and Bible schools. Others of us teach in Religious Education/CCD (Confraternity of Christian Doctrine)—a program of education involving volunteers in the Roman Catholic Church. Some of us are called catechists and stand in that early church tradition of introducing persons into the life of the church. In China we might be called "Bible persons"—those who open up the Scriptures to anyone who walks through an open church door. In some places we might be a village elder, a tribal chief, or the grandmother of a family clan. Many of us are ordained or consecrated to ministries of teaching. Most of us are called laity.

Some of us are new teachers and do not know what is expected of us. Others among us have taught for five, ten, or even twenty or more years. We teach in classrooms, church sanctuaries, and homes. We teach in

12

community gathering places, over the radio, and on T.V. We may teach on Sunday or any other day or evening of the week. We may teach for thirty minutes, for two hours, or all day long.

No matter how many differences there are in the places or approaches to our teaching, we share at least three things in common: (a) we belong to the fellowship of those committed to the gospel of Jesus Christ as the creative and reconciling word for all people; (b) we share the commission of Jesus Christ to teach that all may become disciples; and (c) we are volunteers. In other words, we are not paid to teach, and in some way, we also participated in the decision that led to our becoming teachers.

CHAPTER 1

The Volunteer Teacher Is Called

Even a superficial reading of the Bible reveals that God uses many approaches to involve people in ministries of creation and reconciliation. Moses, Isaiah, and Paul had dramatic encounters with the holiness of God that revealed for them specific tasks to fulfill the will of God. God's purposes for Jeremiah and John the Baptist seemed to have been evident before they were born. For several of the disciples, friendship with Jesus preceded a clear sense of mission. The love and teachings of mother and grandmother nurtured Timothy into God's service. Those of us who teach today also came to that ministry by many routes.

Some of us are teaching because we have felt we were personally led by God into that ministry. We have responded to an inner urging that would not let us go until we responded. We may have had a sign that indicated that to be a disciple of Jesus Christ involved the responsibility of teaching. We may have come to this awareness through a dramatic experience or it may have quietly and persistently pushed its way into our consciousness. Whatever the character of our experience, it became clear that if we were to be faithful to the leading of the Holy Spirit, we would be teaching. In this way we share the urgency to follow God's will that we see in the prophetic work of Isaiah or Paul.

Some of us were recruited to teach. Jesus went through the countryside inviting one after another to follow him. In a similar fashion, pastors, directors of Christian education, age group superintendents and coordinators, other teachers, members of recruiting committees, or perhaps even a group of children or youth may have written us a letter, called us on the phone, or visited in our homes. They described a need. They identified the resources we would have. They challenged or persuaded us. We agreed to become a teacher in the church. But our reasons for accepting that invitation may well have been mixed. I have talked with volunteer teachers who began teaching because they liked the person who asked them. They did not know how to say "no." Others agreed to teach because they enjoyed working with a given age group. Still others simply liked to teach and welcomed the opportunity. Some responded because they felt a sense of duty. It was their turn even though they may have disliked or were afraid of the task. Another group jumped at the chance to teach because it provided an opportunity to share with others the joy they experienced in their own relationship to God. I have also met teachers who accepted the responsibility because they knew they could do a better job than anyone else who was available. Their commitment to the quality of the educational experience compelled them to accept the invitation. And others simply accepted so that they might learn more about the beliefs and values of the church. In one sense, it really does not make much difference how we were asked or what our motivations or feelings were when we agreed to teach. When meeting a class or group for the first time, we came as a representative of the church to share in Christ's teaching ministry.

Some of us volunteered for the task. Some among us did not wait until we were invited to teach. We offered ourselves. Again the reasons for our decision to teach may vary. For many volunteers it has to do with the love of teaching or the enjoyment received in working with a given age group. It may be rooted in a deep commitment to share with others the Christian story and experience. It may be that we saw a weakness or an empty place in the church's ministry and saw no one else to fill it. We did not wait, however, for someone to recognize our concern, commitment, interest, or skills. We simply made ourselves available to the person administering the congregation's or the parish's educational program.

Still others among us stumbled into teaching. As I remember my own experience, I began teaching while in high school. If I recall the situation correctly, I was sitting with my high school classmates waiting for our session to begin. The Sunday school superintendent started to walk by but then stopped to ask me if I would be willing to meet with the junior boys that morning. Their teacher had not shown up. Apparently the teacher never showed up, because I stopped teaching that class when I left for college two years later. I know many teachers who began by helping their mothers or by agreeing to substitute for the teachers of their own classes. Without a clear decision on their part, they became teachers and discovered in it a significant expression of their involvement in the church's ministry. In a sense, they "stumbled," much as I did, into this important ministry.

Still others among us teach because our place in the community includes that responsibility. The task involves no remuneration and in that sense is voluntary. But it was not freely chosen. In many towns and villages in the United States in years past, it was assumed that public school teachers would also teach in the Sunday school. In those two roles they provided continuity between civic and religious instruction. In many tribal villages around the world, the chief or head of the family is designated by tradition to be the teacher of religious and moral values and practices. Similarly, in many small congregations an older member is viewed by everyone else as the person to tell the stories of faith and to make sure that the children and youth learn to act in ways consistent with Christian beliefs and values. Pastors, priests, and directors of Christian education often find that they are looked upon as primary teachers in their congregations or parishes. It is not personal interest, skill, or commitment, but the expectation of the community that prompts such people to teach.

Not all of us accepted the task of teaching with enthusiasm. Nor did all of us burn with the desire that compelled Paul to teach and preach whenever and wherever he found someone who would listen. Indeed if we are honest, many of us probably would prefer to be doing something else. We try to minimize the work involved or resist the expectations of the church or parish staff. We long to stay at home. We criticize the resources for making the job seem harder than we think it needs to be. We make excuses for our work. When we step back and look at our thoughts, however, we discover that through the ages those whom God has called have responded in similar ways. Some of us share the fear of Moses that we are not capable of doing what God has asked of us. Some of us are like Jonah. We try to hide from the responsibilities, yet somehow we cannot escape them. Some of us are burdened by the apathy and resistance of those we teach. But then so were Elijah, Jeremiah, Jesus, the disciples, and the apostles. Some of us would prefer to be sitting at the feet of a good teacher ourselves, yet we share Martha's sense of duty and go about our tasks because they have to be done. God uses us, in other words, often in spite of ourselves.

No matter how we became a volunteer teacher, from God's perspective *we have all been called into this ministry*. The call of God is not reserved for those who become ordained. The call is the means by which God engages all people in ministry. The experience of God's call is as common as the bread and wine used in the celebration of the Lord's Supper. It is also as special as the experience of Holy Communion. James Dunning has reminded us that our call to ministry may be traced to the fact that we were created in the image of God. In baptism we take on the responsibility of being the bearers of God's image. It is our vocation to witness to the presence of God stamped into our very being. For some of us, teaching is the way we share that presence with others.[3]

We come to our awareness of the way we will be God's presence to others in a variety of ways. This awareness or "call" can be as dramatic as Isaiah's vision in the temple or as ordinary as a boy being asked to share his lunch of bread and fish with those who had none. The extraordinary consequences of his response only dramatize the fact that none of us can predict the outcome of our response to the initiative to serve God and others.

Most of us received the call to teach through some common and ordinary channel of God's grace. We saw a need and responded. We were elected to the office. We were asked to teach by someone from the congregation or parish. Sometimes this followed a careful analysis of church needs and our leadership skills. Sometimes it was the action of a church officer trying to fill a vacancy. These efforts may all look like the ongoing work of the organizational church. As the body of Christ, however, the congregation or parish through its committees and procedures is probably the most common instrument of God's call. It is a point Paul made in his letter to the troubled Corinthian church. As members of the church we are the body of Christ. We are each a part of that body. We have a place and a task in that body. In spite of our human tamperings with church structure, it is God who has determined that there shall be apostles, prophets, and teachers. It is through the structures of church life that we are named to those responsibilities and then assume them. They may seem ordinary and flawed to us, but those very familiar structures for recruiting and organizing a local parish or congregation are among the most common channels for God's grace. In this sense our response to the invitation to teach becomes an expression of our involvement in the larger ministry of the church as the body of Christ. Teaching does not become an extra job, or an additional time commitment. It becomes an outlet for expressing our loyalty to the one who created and redeemed us.

If you would like, use the following questions to reflect on your call to teaching.

1. When did you begin teaching? _____

2. Did you feel led into teaching? _____ Were you recruited? _____ Did you volunteer? _____
   Did you "stumble" into teaching? _____
   Was it part of another role or responsibility? _____
3. What happened? _____
   _____
   _____

4. How do you feel about being a volunteer teacher? _____
   _____

5. Can you think of people in the Bible who had similar feelings about their responsibilities? If so, who? _____
   How did their feelings affect the way their work was evaluated by the biblical writer?
   _____
   _____

6. What difference does it make to think of yourself as being "called" to teach, no matter how you became a teacher? _____
   _____
   _____

CHAPTER 2

The Volunteer Teacher Is Gifted

One of the most powerful themes in Paul's writings emphasizes that the work of the Holy Spirit is the source of those gifts that enable people to carry on the work of being Christ's body in the world. When we are called to teach, those gifts are lifted up, consecrated if you will, for the welfare of all. In the historic language of the church, the gifts we bring to our teaching are blessed. It is not so much that certain gifts are prerequisite for effective teaching, but that the gifts we already possess are sanctioned as channels for the grace of God. Perhaps this theme is evident in the lines that follow:

Among those who teach
There are many different gifts
But the same Spirit gives them all;
There are different abilities required of those who teach,
But God gives what is needed to fulfill that ministry.
There are different approaches to teaching
But the same God is served through them all;
The Spirit's presence is revealed through those who teach for the benefit of all.
The Spirit gives to one person the power to tell stories of God's reconciling love, while to another, the ability to interpret stories.
It is the same Spirit who gives to one person the gift of asking penetrating questions and to another, the gift of discerning the future in a student's answers.
To one is given the ability to recognize and touch with healing the pain in people's lives, and to another, the ability to challenge apathy and hypocrisy with words of hope and faith.
The Spirit gives one person the power to see into the mystery of God; to another, the capacity to envision the kingdom of God, and to still another, the wisdom to discern the mystery of God's work in the common and routine events in our lives.
The Spirit gives to one the skills for effective speaking; to another, the sensitivity for significant caring; and to still another, the creativity to stimulate reflective thought and faithful action.
Those who teach have diverse gifts
but it is the same Spirit who gives them all, who works in and through all who teach to the glory of God and the benefit of all.

(Based on I Corinthians 12:4-11)

I do not know what your gifts are, but through the Spirit they have been blessed as special means for the teaching ministry. This insight may help make us into inspired and competent teachers. Instead of waiting foolishly for a miracle, we may be able to concentrate on the tasks at hand, using and refining the gifts we already possess. These gifts are the source of our blessing and the means of God's grace. Using our gifts as a sign of our own commitment to Christ as head of the church, we serve as the hands, feet, legs, and eyes of Christ for others. We embody, or make specific, Christ's ministry. We have been called and now we are teachers.

As I write these words, the description of Jesus sending the seventy out into the villages to preach and to heal comes to mind. If all seventy had the variety of gifts found among the twelve, what a diverse group of talents and abilities Jesus acknowledged to be useful in ministry! Of course they were no more diverse than are the gifts we bring to our own teaching. Probably the seventy were no more surprised than we are when people encounter the liveliness of God's word through us. We all too often forget that when we put our gifts to God's use, that it is not we, but God, who makes use of them. In the process they are no longer ordinary. They become the means for God's working.

I am reminded of the woman whose respect for the curiosity of older children and whose appreciation for her own musical talents transformed a traditional unit of church history into an exciting venture. Who would have thought that a musical approach to history could become the basis for almost perfect attendance in that class? I also think of a man who was very self-conscious when talking about matters of faith in a classroom or meeting, but who had no difficulty teaching while working with children or adults on some mechanical project. It is obvious that intellectual curiosity, knowledge, and love are gifts to be found in effective teachers. Less obvious are those times when people offer their shyness, handicaps, and lack of knowledge or creativity to God and discover in the process that those apparent stumbling blocks became the means through which God works. When shyness helps a teacher listen or a handicap encourages a student's initiative, amazing things happen to those in the teaching-learning situation. When we teach, whatever we bring has the potential to be blessed as a gift to enrich the quality of our teaching. I consider that good news.

The Ministry of the Volunteer Teacher

If you would like, use the following questions to reflect on your gifts for teaching.

1. Identify at least five gifts that you bring to the ministry of teaching.

   _____

   _____

2. Identify a time when one or two of those gifts contributed to the religious growth of person(s) in your class. _____

   _____

   _____

3. In a sentence or two, talk about how your gifts may contribute to Christ's ministry of teaching._____

   _____

PART II

The Responsibility of the Volunteer Teacher

Introduction

Walter Brueggemann has said it well. Education is a community concern. When people with a common identity take education seriously, they intend for their congregation, denomination, or nation "to last over the generations." Education is concerned with maintaining "enough continuity of vision, value, and perception" to sustain a specific community's identity over time. It is, at the same time, concerned with providing enough "freedom and novelty" to respond to the threat to its existence posed by the challenge of new events and circumstances.[1] Education, in other words, is crucial both for the survival and the relevance of a community. I have said it before, but it is worth repeating here. Education prevents the extinction of a community and the relegation of its ideals, institutions, and artifacts to museums and history books. Education, moreover, keeps a community on the growing edge of the future, shaping the destiny of its people out of the interplay of the community's heritage and its new possibilities.

Perhaps it is no surprise, then, that Paul should so highly value the work of the teacher. Although there are clearly educational consequences in the work of prophets, priests, and apostles, it is the teacher who assumes the crucial responsibility for mediating a community's past and its future. The teacher participates in what Brueggemann has called "the construction of a world."[2] It is a world rooted in the values and images of the past, but it is a world that draws each present generation into the future.

What then is the social responsibility of the teacher? I would like to suggest that there are three major functions that teachers fulfill in maintaining the life of any community, including that of a congregation or parish. Although individual teachers may have the gifts or interests to do only one of them, if all three are not present in the educational work of a congregation or parish, that congregation or parish is in danger of becoming irrelevant as an agency of God's work in the world.

CHAPTER 3

The Responsibility to Bind the Generations

Several years ago, while serving a congregation as its minister of Christian education, I became aware of some unusual excitement in the four- and five-year-old church school class. The season was Advent. The teachers were seeking for a fresh way to introduce the Christmas story and decided to have the children act out the story while the teachers told it. This activity meant they could make use of a box of biblical costumes in children's sizes someone had made several years before. On the first Sunday of Advent they gave each child a role to be acted out and a costume. They then *told* the story while the children lived out the familiar roles in that story. The consequence was more than the teachers anticipated. As soon as the story was over, several children immediately asked if they could do it again and have a different role. Each child, it seems, wanted to be Mary or Joseph. So the teachers promised to repeat the activity the following week. The pattern had been set. They ended up telling the story with different children in the various roles each of the Sundays of Advent as well as on Christmas Sunday morning.

This incident is not unusual. As I have shared it with teachers across the country, it usually brings to mind similar experiences for them. Its familiarity, however, may reveal several things about the function of teachers in the community of faith. Let us return to that story and note what those teachers did.

1. *They re-created a primary event in our faith history.* In this case it was simply done. It involved the telling of a story—one of the most powerful ways of inviting people into the meaning and experience of others. In this case both the format of storytelling and the story were familiar. The children knew what was expected of them. At one level they were to listen to the story and to the cues in the story for taking their place in the nativity scene. At another level they were to let their imaginations soar and to play with the idea that they were, in fact, Mary, Joseph, the innkeeper, or one of the shepherds. This structured and familiar activity gave them room to enter into one of the most moving and profound events in Christian history. This learning activity, in other words, shortened the distance between the present and an event two thousand years ago. It revealed the continuing power of that event to grip the imagination and the faith of a group of children and teachers today. Such is the power of a story. But the re-creation of significant events can also take place through the use of a wide variety of traditional teaching strategies. Drama and the arts may be obvious examples. The use of research and the sharing of that research through lecture, discussion, or a variety of other methods, however, can also become the means of entering into the drama of the interaction of

God and our faith ancestors. These activities, of course, reveal the vitality and relevance of our heritage for our own experience.

2. *The teachers responded to the children's questions:* "Can I be Mary?" "Can I be Joseph?" "Could I be the donkey?" At one level these questions simply have to do with being able to try on a costume or to have the opportunity to be at the center of the stage. At another level these same questions involve much deeper meanings: "Can I see Jesus as Mary might have seen him?" "Can I experience what was going on in Joseph's mind?" At this level Brueggemann observes that our teaching is a response to the child's "yearning to belong" to the people into which he or she was born or adopted. That yearning is located in the desire of children and newcomers to know the secrets that distinguish their family, their congregation or parish, or their nation from other people.[3] For example, no matter what our age, none of us can really understand the Incarnation until we begin to ponder the mystery of those events in the manner of Mary. We cannot begin to grasp the demands of the Incarnation until we recognize the significance of finding food and shelter for those we love in the midst of unexplainable circumstances in the manner of Joseph. We cannot begin to grasp the wonder of the Incarnation until we can walk in the shoes of shepherds or wise men to the plain places of life and see God there. It is in those places that we discover the "secrets" that distinguish the Christian experience. In the answers of a teacher to a student's questions, the teacher may open up and make available to the student what it means to bear the identity of the Christian community. At the same time, the teacher may help the student recognize his or her own encounters with the mystery of God.

3. The story not only precipitated the children's questions. The *teachers repeated the story*—over and over again. The children were not told about the story. They did not receive a list of rules for living the Christian life. Instead they were invited to participate in the rehearsal of that story until it was firmly planted in their memories and imaginations. In this incident the children did know best. In their requests to have the story told again and again, they remind us that the power of a story in our lives is dependent upon its familiarity.

This rather common incident may point to one of the primary responsibilities of teachers: *to bind the generations.* I am indebted to Brueggemann again for this phrase.[4] It is a more dynamic way of describing the processes of handing on the faith from one generation to the next than "transmitting" or "socialization." It embodies those actions creating a sense of solidarity among the generations. The old are able to envision a future in the dreams of the young, and the young can see themselves carrying the community's heritage into the unknown of that future. The point is clearly stated in the expectation of the hymnist that the faith of our fathers and mothers lives on in us, enlivening our imaginations, feeding our dreams, and challenging our disobedience. It reminds us that the uniqueness of our individual personalities is insignificant when compared with the bonds we share with people to whom we belong.[5] Teachers seek to make familiar both the stories of the community's past and the values, hopes, and ways of behaving that distinguish our people from other people. In that process the teacher helps students discover the relevance of their past for their future and their dependence upon the "saints" of the past for clues to cope with the challenges of the future. In this sense, teachers intensify the bond of people across the generations.

CHAPTER 4

The Responsibility to Build Up the Community of Faith to Glorify God and to Serve Neighbor

Every community has a reason for its existence. So does the church and every congregation or parish that makes up the church. When we look at any given congregation or parish we may see many purposes reflected in its activities, its stewardship of resources, and its attitudes toward the world around it. But underneath these purposes we encounter the primary reason for the church's existence: to glorify God and to serve our neighbors. This twofold commandment, first expressed in the Deuteronomic law and later by Jesus as the core of the faithful life, is familiar to all of us. But it often is not obvious to us in the way the church approaches its educational responsibilities. If people do learn to worship (the corporate way we glorify God), it is usually by chance. Most of us learned the hymns, prayers, and creeds simply by participating in corporate worship. We learned the postures of worship (standing, kneeling, sitting) by following the lead of those around us. Perhaps we also learned to hear the Word of God in the midst of these activities. Most of us, however, are probably still like the boy Samuel. When we hear the voice of God we cannot distinguish it from the words of our worship leaders, preachers, and teachers. It is the teacher's task, as it was Eli's, to help point to the difference.

I am reminded of the leader of a highly disciplined religious community who did not want visitors to participate actively in the liturgy because their ignorance and lack of skill in the way worship was done in that place would diminish the quality of the gift of daily praise and thanksgiving. He was right, of course. People who do not know how to worship diminish the quality of the church's acts of praise and thanksgiving. We may not like what he did. He was excluding people. And yet, it is strange that we do not see anything out of the ordinary about exercising the same judgment in an athletic contest. No partisan crowd would want a coach to send in a player who had little sense of the spirit of the team (the binding described earlier), who was not physically and emotionally in good condition, and who did not know the plays to the point that he or she could do them without wondering what to do next. Yet all too many parishes and congregations rarely recognize the necessity of appropriate physical, spiritual, relational, and missional conditioning for worship. We need to be taught how to give glory with all our being.

If we learn to serve our neighbors at the point of their needs, it also tends to be by happenstance. Our efforts to reach the poor, the outcast, and the victims of injustice are corrupted by our ignorance, our paternalism, and our own self-interest. To engage in such ministries of love and justice or to reach out to share the good news of Jesus Christ involves seeing more than the needs of others. It begins with seeing Christ in and through those whom we seek to serve. Our service to others, in other words, becomes not a way to share the bounty of our personal resources or the excitement of our own experience of Christ's love. Instead it is in our service to our neighbor that we serve the Christ. In that act we also glorify the God who created us brother and sister.

The ministry of teaching in the church is concerned with being faithful to the God who creates, calls, and sends. In this way teachers help build up the body of Christ to glorify God and to serve neighbor. To give God glory is to love and serve neighbor. To serve neighbor as we have been served by Christ is to glorify God. These two actions are necessarily interdependent. The acquisition of knowledge is an obvious by-product of this effort. So is the development of moral values or social justice. Such teaching is not anti-intellectual, valueless, or uninterested in justice. Indeed, the opposite is true. To give God glory is to begin to view the world from the vantage point of God's perspective. All the knowledge of God is the subject of our teaching. The character of God sets the standards for our teaching. And the righteousness of God undergirds the vision for the effect of our teaching in the lives of persons and on the world.

It is at this point that teachers contribute uniquely to the mission of the church. Their concern is *to train the members of a community to use the resources that are basic to the actions of praise and service.* Just as with any task certain things must be known, certain attitudes must be nurtured, certain behaviors must be refined, certain skills must be developed, and certain standards must be established if a community of faith is to fulfill its purposes. In a sense we are describing the concern for mastery or competency to be found in the literature on education but with at least one distinguishing fact. Most discussions on mastery or competence emphasize the knowledge or skills of the individual. In the church the emphasis is necessarily upon corporate competence.

Paul made the same point. We are members one of another—one body—one people. The fulfillment of our own ministry is dependent upon the effectiveness of all our ministries. We are as strong as all the parts are strong. Our weakness is to be found in the weakness of our parts. Our worship is diminished if the word proclaimed is superficial or irrelevant, if the music lacks rhythm, if the fellowship is torn by jealousy or strife, if the hearing is blunted by ignorance. Our service to others is thwarted if we are blind to the pain in the lives of others, if our own self-centeredness creates in us hardness of heart, if we are naïve about the way political and economic institutions work.

When I conduct workshops for teachers and other educational leaders in local churches I often ask the participants: "What would you want a person to know or be able to do after ten or twelve years in your church's education program?" I have not yet been in a group that had ever raised this question for itself. How can one build up a community for worship and service when we have not thought through what is basic to those actions? I am intrigued, however, by the responses to a second set of questions I also usually ask: "What Bible stories do most people in your congregation over ten years of age know?" "What hymns are sung most frequently?" "When people reach out to others in need, what pain or problem attracts their attention?" These and other questions usually reveal that unconsciously most congregations and parishes can readily identify several scripture passages, doctrines, hymns, and prayers that embody the core of their faith commitments. They also emphasize the development of certain skills as marks of the faithful person in both worshiping God and responding to the needs of others. These are signs of a congregation's or parish's faithfulness. But they may also tend to limit our awareness of the variety of God's creative and redemptive activity. There are times when I feel some people and some congregations have reduced the gospel to the parable of the prodigal son, or to the parables of final judgment, or to the injunction to have dominion over all the earth without attending to the whole of the gospel. Such a community is not being built up as a part of the *body* of Christ.

Teaching is that function of ministry that challenges our very human tendency to limit our knowledge and skills to that which is familiar or manageable. Instead *teachers engage people in activities to appropriate the knowledge, attitudes, and skills crucial to the work of the community* as the body of Christ.

The important words in the preceding sentence are "crucial to the work." Tom Groome has introduced a technical theological phrase into the discussions on religious education that is useful here. He has convincingly described the teaching-learning event as "shared praxis." He means simply that when a group of Christians reflects upon an event or experience in their lives they must (1) make use of the resources for understanding that event or experience from both the community's faith heritage and its vision of the future and (2) act upon the decisions they reach in the midst of that study. This means the teacher is simultaneously concerned with *training* persons for, *engaging* persons in, and *reflecting* with persons on the meaning of their involvement in worship and service. Each step is crucial to the task of building up the community of faith.

This may be a new way of describing what teachers do, but the process is familiar to most of us. For example, a child wants to bake cookies. A parent reads through the recipe with the child and then supervises the way the child measures and mixes the various ingredients. This is *training*. But it is also *engagement*. The child is doing the work. When the first batch of cookies is taken from the oven, they are tasted as soon as they are cool enough. If the parent leads the child in a discussion of taste, texture, and baking time, they can reflect on how they had done their task in anticipation of the next time they would bake cookies.

When our daughter was learning to play string bass she had a similar experience. Each spring she and her junior high peers practiced or trained for several weeks for the joint concert with the city's senior high and professional orchestras. On the appointed day, each orchestra played several selections. But the last part was the high point of the concert. All three orchestras played together with young musicians interspersed among their professional counterparts. This concert *engaged* the student musicians in a common task with the standards and quality of the adult orchestra setting the pace. During the rehearsal after the concert, the conductor/teacher looked back at the experience and *reflected* with them on what they needed to know and do to be a more effective orchestral group in the future.

So it is with the way some teachers in the church approach their work. I am reminded of the bicycle shop, a class for fifth and sixth graders that merged denominational curricular goals with the restoration of used bicycles for children who had none. A large garage next to the church building became the headquarters for this lively group to sing, pray, read, and get their hands greasy. The "pay-off" of this experience occurred when the city was devastated by flood waters. One of the teachers of the class supervised those same boys and girls in repairing small appliances damaged by mud and water. Their usefulness to the community was obvious to all. Again their teachers *trained* them both to repair bicycles and to see themselves as agents of Christ's reconciling work. They *engaged* in a ministry to others and discussed or *reflected* upon the relationship of their efforts to the church's historic commitment to respond to those in need.

26

In the building up of the community, the teacher's attention is directed to the *usefulness* of its members to the work of the community. Do the students have the knowledge and skills needed to participate in the community's acts of worship and service? The teacher's attention, moreover, is directed to the *quality* of the student's work in fulfilling those tasks central to the mission of the community. To this end they establish guidelines and standards for their efforts. And, perhaps surprisingly, the teacher's attention is also directed to the development of skills for *coping with the disruptive experiences* that often accompany obedient servanthood. This last set of tasks is mindful of the fact that the people of God often find themselves standing against the values, goals, and practices of the larger society. At this point teachers wonder if their students are secure enough in the community's faith in the sovereignty of God to withstand such challenges. In summary, teachers are responsible for the preparation of persons to participate effectively in the actions of worship and service that both identify and reveal the faith of the Christian community in the world.

CHAPTER 5

The Responsibility to Instruct for Faithful Discipleship and Responsible Living

One of the most dramatic moments of my ministry occurred back in the 1960s when it was popular for congregations to sponsor coffee houses for the youth of the community. Our youth fellowship had transformed the loft of a carriage house on church property into a rustic gathering place for young people. In keeping with their image of a coffee house, cable drums had been used for tables and old wagon wheels had been transformed into light fixtures.

On one crowded Saturday night a teenager who had had too much beer to drink slipped by the watchful eyes of the adult supervisors. In a moment of bravado he jumped on one of the tables and tried to swing from a wagon wheel light fixture. Since it was not designed to hold that much weight, the fixture and he came tumbling down. Miraculously, no one was hurt. Such an event is always a shock to a group. The police heard about it and came to check out the story. Church leaders heard about it and called the pastor to verify it. Some suggested strongly that the coffee house should be closed. The young people were frightened by the close call and angered by the disruption this young man's behavior had caused in their efforts to be in ministry to the youth of the community.

The youth leaders and counselors set aside their plans for the Sunday evening youth fellowship program to discuss their response to the situation. What should they say on Monday when they saw the young man in school? How were they to react to the increasing pressure of a growing number of people in the church to close the place? Was there a way to improve supervision? Was the popularity of the coffee house a sign of their ministry or had it become an end in itself? It was a somber meeting as the young people waded through these and other questions and their ethical, theological, and practical consequences. Faced with the prospect of a called meeting of the church board to discuss the coffee house, the president pushed for a rationale for the decisions of the youth fellowship. At this point the counselors began to explore the issues from an explicitly biblical perspective. They began to shift from the language of judgment to the language of redemption.

Later while facing the church board, the president described the group's decision to keep the coffee house open, to tighten supervision, and to invite the young man back as long as he was sober and attentive to the safety regulations of the coffee house. She located their decisions squarely in the importance of forgiveness as the occasion for life-changing decisions. As one man later said, these young people reminded us of what the church should be about.

In this incident, the almost invisible actions of the youth counselors illustrate at least three ways that teachers *instruct others for faithful living and responsible discipleship*—a third responsibility of teachers.

1. They helped the youth fellowship to face up to the responsibilities of membership in the body of Christ. As the "managers" of a public place, the young people were responsible for the experience and the welfare of all who came. As agents of the church's ministry to others, they were responsible for the stewardship of the physical and personnel resources of the church. They were accountable for the character of the gospel communicated to the whole community by their decisions and actions. Although the incident had legal and moral ramifications that many thought the youth fellowship too inexperienced to handle, the counselors insisted that the fellowship must struggle with the critical problems, as well as the pleasures, of sponsoring the coffee house as an expression of the church's ministry. They helped the young people realize that their actions had both religious and ethical consequences.

2. The youth leaders did not let the discussion end until the young people could begin to make sense out of the incident. For Christians, this means being able to understand any life experience in the light of the gospel. Just as the mission of Jesus became clear to many in the early church in their reading of the messianic passages of Isaiah, we also may discover deeper insight into our own life situations as we encounter ourselves in the Scriptures. It really means the gospel sheds light on who we are and what we are doing. Like a candle in a dark room, it can help reveal both our motivations and the meaning of our actions.

This process is often called an interpretive one. It involves two steps. By looking at them together, we may come to understand each better. For example, if we were to try to understand what might be expected of us if we had been in the shoes of those teenagers as they pondered what to do, and if we were also confronted by the injunction to "love one another as I have loved you," what would be our response? If we take both the boy and the biblical imperative seriously we could not ignore the boy or the imperative. We could not say "boys will be boys." We could not close the coffee house to all but proven Christians. We could not really ask the church council to get us out of this mess. We would have to find a response faithful to the gospel and relevant to the situation. This interpretive process is a common task for teachers. Teachers are confronted by it every time a couple of five-year-olds get into a fight or a group of adults affirms the importance of caring for those who are hurting but then refuses to extend compassion to a couple in the class going through a painful divorce.

When James Smart wrote of the "strange silence of the Bible" in the churches, he was pointing in part to the lack of teachers engaging students in this responsibility. The consequence may be found in congregations and parishes whose ministries are apathetic and irrelevant. It may be seen in the way congregations and parishes reflect or mirror popular values in the culture. It may also be seen in the way some congregations equate the totality of the gospel with their own commitments to that gospel.

3. The leaders in this incident also provided a place where the youth group could explore and examine optional responses to the situation before making a decision to act. They set aside the existing program of the youth group, and a committee called everyone to spread the word about the change of plans and the new agenda. The leaders set up the chairs in a big circle so that all present might feel they had permission to add their points of view. They also reminded the young people that all decisions had to be reviewed by the administrative council of the congregation.

This meeting provided an opportunity for the youth group "to get its act together" within the established structures and procedures governing congregational life. Time apart for sorting

29

through feelings and thoughts is crucial in any decision-making situation—especially one that has the air of crisis about it. That time is also important if making decisions is to be a vehicle for growth in wisdom, understanding, and stature in the community of faith. And it is no less important in the quiet everyday sessions that make up most of our teaching experience.

In every session we have the opportunity to help those we teach discover the power in our faith heritage for making decisions about how to live into the future. That is the task of binding past, present, and future generations into a continuing witness to the redemptive work of God.

In every session we have the opportunity to involve children, teenagers, and adults in activities that build up the church for the purposes of glorifying God and serving our neighbor.

In every session we have the opportunity to instruct those we teach in the knowledge, attitudes, and skills basic to lives of faithful discipleship and responsible living.

These three tasks are central to our work no matter what age group we might teach. It is also true that few of us can effectively fulfill all three responsibilities. That is one reason why every congregation and parish has a community of teachers. Together we share the responsibilities for teaching in the community of faith. Together we reinforce our strengths and reduce the problems located in our limitations. Together we carry forward the church's ministry to teach.

IF you would like to explore your contribution to the teaching ministry, complete the following questions:

1. What was the most important insight you received from reading this chapter?_____

_____

2. Which of the three responsibilities of teachers described in this chapter do you fulfill most effectively? Which the least effectively?

    Bind the generations————

    Build up the church for ministries of praise and service————

    Instruct for faithful discipleship————

3. Give an example of the responsibility you fulfill most effectively.

    _____

    _____

    _____

4. What one thing could you do to be even more effective in fulfilling this responsibility?

    _____

PART III

The Work of the Volunteer Teacher: To Create an Environment of Caring

Introduction

When Paul drew up his list of the ministries of the church he did not define them or distinguish one from another. Perhaps the differences as well as the interdependence of prophesying, teaching, healing and the rest seemed obvious to him. Perhaps he recognized the diversity in each which makes it difficult to describe in a few simple words what prophets or teachers really do to fulfill their responsibilities for the community of faith. Perhaps he understood the influences that background, training, and personality have on the way we undertake our responsibilities. Yet he and we do make a distinction between the tasks of preaching, teaching, organizing, and healing which contribute to the life and mission of the church.

The next two sections clarify what teachers do. I would like to suggest that teachers have two primary tasks. The first involves creating a setting that supports and reinforces our efforts to serve as the mediators of the vision and values of the historic Christian community for the future. I call this work the creation of a caring environment. The second has to do with the task of teaching itself. This task is concerned with planning to introduce and incorporate persons into what it means to be members of the community of faith we call the body of Christ.

In this next section we will explore the first of these tasks by examining three different ways teachers can help create a caring environment. This task is based on the premise that the grace of God undergirds, surrounds, and fills the teaching-learning enterprise of the church. We certainly cannot presume to control or direct the grace of God, but we can help generate what my friend and colleague Everett Tilson has called an environment of grace. We can undertake the task of being open to the leading of the Holy Spirit in our own teaching. We can nurture relationships of love among those we teach. We can help structure experiences that reveal the presence and power of God's love. This task is crucial in that it nurtures a receptiveness on our part to the love and care of God. It also helps to develop in us a sensitivity and responsiveness to others.

You may find elements of all three of the following suggestions for creating a caring environment already present in your teaching. You may also find that some of the things that go on in your classes actually prevent a caring environment from developing. Perhaps this discussion will provide some clues to strengthen the openness of all of us to the work of God in our midst.

The Task of Making God's Care Visible

One way to create an environment of caring is to make visible God's care for those we teach. Perhaps because I have worked with educational ministries of local churches for more than twenty years, I find I can now tell much about what goes on in a classroom by walking into it when no one else is present. The arrangement of the chairs or desks often provides clues about the relationships of people in that place. A large desk in the front and center of the room conveys one picture about the way a teacher relates to students. The absence of any special place for the teacher gives a different picture. The location of pictures and maps, the content and quality of the work of students displayed on the walls, and the way the resources used in class time are stored all provide clues to what is valued in that place. These things all send messages about what might be happening when teachers and students meet. They make visible, before we speak, messages about the way we as teachers and churches communicate God's care for those we teach and how important we think the task of teaching really is.

I remember walking into a room of an affluent congregation where three-year-olds met with their teacher. The tiny chairs were placed in narrow rows before an altar table so high that most children would have had to step on their tiptoes to see over it. The room was painted a dark gray-green. There were no pictures on the walls. The supplies were locked in a closet. There were no tables. Although the teacher may have had a good relationship with the children, the sterility of the room did not help build it.

I have seen classes for older adults up long flights of steps or in damp and drafty basement rooms. I've been intrigued by the number of congregations and parishes that put their teenagers in rooms as far away from the primary flow of traffic in the church building as possible. Again, the interaction of teachers and students may have been healthy and vigorous, but the placement of their rooms also conveyed negative messages about the congregation's or parish's view of the contribution of older adults and young people to its life.

In one church building I discovered the infant nursery located in the basement next to the furnace room. A simple plaster and lathe wall divided the two rooms. A single attendant often cared for as many as ten children during the worship services of the congregation. Apparently no one had thought about the potential danger this situation posed for the children.

In many classrooms I have seen attendance charts on the wall with stars marking the presence of children. Some names had stars below each date on the chart. Other names had several stars at the beginning of the chart, then a few stars in the middle, and almost no stars at the end. Still other names had only one or two stars in all. Attendance in these classes was obviously highly valued. A corresponding message may well be that if a person does not attend regularly, he or she is not as accepted as others. One has to prove one's worth by attendance. The valued members have many stars. Less valued members have fewer stars. For some people, however, regular attendance may be impossible. Children of divorced parents, for example, often cannot be consistently present due to custody agreements. To be considered an important and valued group member would be difficult for such a child.

So far I have only mentioned negative examples of what John Westerhoff has called the "hidden curriculum" in any educational setting. A hidden curriculum, of course, also can reinforce positively the intentions we bring to our teaching. For example, I have seen rooms so invitingly set up that children would walk through the door, stop, look around, and let out a long "ohhh" of delight before plunging into a learning activity that caught their attention. I have known teachers who made sure that displays included pictures that reflected the cultural and ethnic diversity of God's people. The ramp beside the stairs lets the handicapped know that their presence has been anticipated. I could identify more, but these examples illustrate the importance of making sure that the place we teach reinforces what we want students to learn.

Perhaps our task becomes clearer when we compare it to the work of a host or hostess. I think of many occasions when we have visited in someone's home. We were greeted warmly. We talked to people who seemed interested in our ideas. We experienced people laughing together rather than at the expense of someone. We felt that we could act naturally. The food was good. The time passed quickly, and we left reluctantly. In those hours we experienced trust, intimacy, joy, and hope. It is no accident that we often associate such moments of graciousness with the graciousness of God. It is an oft-repeated theme in the stories of both Old and New Testaments. For example, Abraham and Sarah welcomed strangers into their home. The widow Zarephath fed the hungry Elijah. The prophets anticipated a magnificent banquet hosted by the messiah for those who had been faithful and righteous. Jesus was received into the homes of a wide variety of people and shared the bounty of their tables.

Henri Nouwen reminds us that this theme is rooted in the Israelite view of hospitality. When we are hospitable, we receive a stranger as a guest; we make him or her feel at home, accepted as a brother or sister. The opposite action to hospitality is hostility. It involves the alienation of the stranger. It is the refusal to welcome the one we do not know well. Often we are not conscious of our acts of hostility. Perhaps that is why it is a common experience of so many people in the church. To put infants in an unprotected room next to the furnace, for example, is a hostile act. To make children who cannot regularly attend a Sunday morning program feel less a part of the group is a hostile act. To place an older-adult class in an upstairs room (if there are alternatives available) may well be a hostile act. The messages in each instance are negative.

The cost of our hostility is high. It prevents the growth of our classes and groups. Social scientists have discovered that the typical volunteer church group usually wants to grow numerically. They would like to experience the vitality that comes with an expanding membership. Their fear of how new members will change a group, however, leads them to say and do things that ensure that very few, if any, visitors will try to join them. We see this dynamic at work among young children and teenagers who often blatantly ignore a visitor. It is also very common among adult groups. I am reminded of someone who said that in spite of having lived in her community for forty years, she was still introduced as a newcomer by many. As a "newcomer" she could not yet be "trusted" with important roles and responsibilities. Her participation in these groups depended more on her persistence than on their acceptance. Few people will try that hard.

Nouwen also points to another loss. He recalls that in both Old and New Testament stories of hospitality, "stranger-guests" bring gifts that may transform the lives of those who take them into their homes. Abraham and Sarah were told by their guests that they would have a son. Along the road to Emmaus two men invited a stranger to share the evening meal with them. As they were eating together, they discovered the gift of the Christ in their midst. From a Christian perspective, acts of hostility cause us to lose the gifts of friendship, peace, hope, love, and new life brought by those who could have been our guests.

In the teaching-learning interaction, I would like to suggest that it is the teacher who serves most often as the host or hostess. It is the teacher who initiates the activities that create the environment to welcome strangers and to make them feel at home. It is the teacher who creates the environment of hospitality and grace. This environment does not require beautiful rooms and fancy equipment. I have experienced hospitable classes in one-room churches and in large, city parishes. I have been graciously received in large and small classes. I have been made to feel at home in classes filled with the latest equipment and all the supplies they could ever use. But I have also known the meaning of being at home in classes of congregations so poor that only the teacher could be given a copy of the curricular resources and there were no supplies available to "enrich" the classroom activities. Money, in other words, does not buy grace. Repeatedly the biblical record emphasizes that it is not the cost or the size of our gifts that counts, but the spirit with which we offer them. The implications for our teaching may be fairly obvious.

There are several things we can do to make our classes hospitable to those who come. If a class is small, the teacher may take responsibility for all of them. If the class is large, the teacher will have to ensure that others assume responsibility. For example, members of the class could be designated or persons could be recruited to assist the teacher with this responsibility. A committee of young people or adults could also establish a climate of caring for all persons who participate in their class or group.

In the first place, we can help create a caring environment by letting *those we teach know they are expected.* I have known some people who always seemed to have the coffee pot on the stove and the cookie jar full—as if they knew we were coming. I have known some teachers and some classes whose warm greetings involved me in the session that followed as if my contribution would make a difference to everyone. In both cases, I was made to feel at home. I counted, whether it was my first visit or my one-hundred-and-first. Several things contributed to this feeling on my part.

In hospitable classes

A place is prepared for those who come. The act of preparing the place for our teaching lets those we teach know that we anticipate their coming. It is much like preparing to have guests for dinner. We clean the house. We set the table. We may choose background music and above all we prepare a meal we think our guests will enjoy. When my wife and I plan a dinner party we usually make out a list of things to do before the guests arrive. Teachers make checklists too. The following list consists of things I try to check before I teach to make sure that students know they are expected. You may have other items to add to your own list. Some items, of course, need to be reviewed only occasionally. Others require our attention every time we teach.

A CHECKLIST TO LET STUDENTS KNOW WE EXPECT THEM

A. Are there signs in the halls or people at the entries to the church building to let newcomers know where the various classes are meeting?

B. Is the room clean?

C. Can everyone get to the room easily? If not, what arrangements need to be made for those who find it difficult?

D. Does any of the furniture need to be repaired? If so, who needs to be contacted to make sure it's safe and usable?

E. Is the temperature comfortable?

F. Are the curricular resources out where we can use them when they are needed?

G. Are the supplies for the teaching activities out where they can be distributed easily when they are needed?

H. Are the pictures, posters, and maps to be used in the session placed where they can be seen easily by everyone?

I. Are any visual aids on the walls posted at the "eye height" of the students?

J. Is there something for students to do that will help them begin to explore the topic for the session as soon as they arrive?

K. Others you would add?

L.

M.

Persons are greeted as they arrive. A favorite New Testament story of most people is that of the prodigal son. Among the reasons for its popularity is the power we sense in the father's waiting and watching for the arrival of his long absent son. Note what the father did. Calling the prodigal "my son," he took him into his arms, and he listened to him. *To call persons by name* as they arrive declares that they belong to this group and in this place. To call persons by name is to enter into relationship with them. *To hug or to shake hands* conveys a sense of closeness and warmth. It means that we respect and value the worth of the other. It means we allow ourselves to be open and vulnerable with them. Even as a formality, a handshake or touch is a sign of being included. *To listen* with compassion conveys a sense of mutuality and trust. The prodigal immediately poured out the story of his waywardness. It is often in listening to others immediately after greeting them that we receive clues to their deepest pain, joys, hurts, and hopes. Especially is this true for children. Perhaps for this reason teachers of larger classes need help with this task—a helper to greet, talk, and listen to people as they arrive.

A second approach to creating an environment of caring is *to make those we teach feel at home.* This is the task of helping those we teach sense that they belong in this place and to the group we teach. It is the task that makes people want to stay after the initial moments of greeting and to return to the next session with the expectation that we look forward to their coming. As I was working on this chapter, my son, a college freshman home for the Thanksgiving break, illustrated the point I am making. Among the first things he did after arriving home was to talk to some of his friends from the church youth group. On Sunday he and his freshman colleagues met at their old senior high school classroom. Later they all returned to the church for the evening youth program and decided to have a college freshman–high school senior get-together the day after Thanksgiving. During the week they spent an evening at the home of a former youth fellowship counselor. This is a fellowship where he and they know they are welcome. What can we as teachers do to help create a similar sense of identification with the fellowship of those we teach?

We can post signs of their belonging. For children this may involve a poster with their pictures and names placed in a conspicuous spot. In classes with large enrollments of youth and adults, permanent name tags with large letters may give every face in the room a name. It is difficult to believe that we belong to a people if they cannot remember our names. We also sense that *we belong to a people and place if we are surrounded by objects that have meaning to us.* I am reminded of friends who always want to show me something when I visit them. They know of a common interest. In sharing it, our relationship is deepened. I am reminded of those teachers who display the work of students so that it can be appreciated by all. Currently I am teaching an adult class in which members bring flowers, plants, wall hangings, and items related to the themes of our study to decorate the room. These gifts heighten the corporate character of our life together. We can also make people feel at home if *they are given an opportunity to speak of things that are important to them.* We all need places where we can tell others about the happenings in our lives and talk about issues and ideas that interest or concern us. Often opportunities for this kind of give-and-take are present in the regular activities of our class sessions. Discussion and other learning activities become the means for the members of the class to offer their own thoughts, ideas, and experiences. In classes that meet for a short time, that emphasize the lecture of the teacher, or that have some members who dominate the conversation, other times and places are needed for the conversations that help people feel at home with a group. For this reason many groups have a coffee hour; others set aside a special time during the class time for sharing important concerns. Social outings, retreats, and monthly dinners may provide still other outlets for people of any age to begin to know each other in the give-and-take of their own conversations and to create a sense of belonging among group members.

A third way we can reveal God's love for those we teach is to *choose activities that respect their interests and abilities.* At this point the teacher faces several problems that often make the teaching task seem impossible.

Ability levels vary. Even in a group of two persons there will be differences in reading, thinking, and artistic and motor skills ability. There will be differences in the sensitivity to the needs of other people and in the capacity to make faith and ethical decisions.

Interests will vary. Any group will have persons with many different interests. We see this in the amount of attention people give to a specific topic or activity. It is evident in the way some groups will divide themselves to talk about the subjects that fascinate them most. Sometimes it is reflected, especially in adult classes when given an option, in the kind of study experience they select. Some will choose in-depth Bible study while others prefer to approach the discussion of faith issues through an examination of contemporary concerns or problems.

The needs of students also differ. Some need affection. Some need to be given room to explore the consequences of their actions. Some need externally imposed limits on their behavior. Some need lots of personal attention. Others need to give attention to others.

Each of us could add other examples to these brief lists of differences in abilities, interests, and needs as we think about the persons we teach. As volunteer teachers, however, we have little control over these differences. They are related to the genetic heritage of each person. They are refined by the social experience in families, school, neighborhoods, and on the job. They are influenced by the physical, human, moral or faith development tasks that consume their attention and energy. They are givens to be accepted.

And yet, it is in the midst of our uniqueness as persons that we as teachers and students encounter the unconditional love of God. We are accepted with the specific abilities, interests, and needs we bring to that relationship. The task for us as teachers then becomes to accept the uniqueness of the persons we teach without being immobilized by our attempts to account for all their differences. It is not an easy task, but I would suggest several principles to use in choosing activities to let those we teach know that we value them and their contribution.

Principle #1

Unless we have lots of help or teach a very small class, we cannot plan activities that will account for all the differences in ability, interest, and need of those we teach. *We have limits to our time and energy, as well as in our own abilities, interests and needs.* These, too, must be taken into consideration.

Principle #2

At the same time *we cannot ignore the different abilities, interests, and needs of those we teach.* They are often gifts that enrich the experience of all. If not received and accepted, those who bring them may well not offer them when they are needed. (This is the experience we have when we ask for a volunteer to make a poster and those who have the ability to do that task do not offer to help. They may be busy. More likely their "gift" was not valued in the past.)

Principle #3

We need to feel comfortable with and excited about the potential of any activity we choose to contribute to the growth in faith and discipleship of those we teach. Our enthusiasm can be contagious. Our expectations for the possibilities in any learning experience influence the expectations of students. We must not be hesitant about leading students into new experiences. If we fail to do so, we confine them to the limits of their own experience.

Principle #4

We need to examine any activity we choose for ways that our students might enter into it. Through this principle we find a way to respond to the tension that is created in us when we are sensitive both to our limits and the variety of needs among those we teach. For too long, teachers have assumed they must find different activities to capture student interests and to make use of student abilities. Since this task is almost impossible, it sets up unrealistic expectations for teachers. There is another way. It is to choose an activity and then ask how the members of a class will be able to participate in it. For example, many teachers ask students to read sections of a curricular resource prior to a discussion of its content. This can be a boring and tedious activity. It clearly discriminates against the poor reader, the hyperactive, the hard of hearing, and, if used extensively, against those who learn best if they can put their thoughts into pictures. But it need not be boring, tedious, or the source of discrimination (another act of hostility). We could contact a poor reader prior to the session to make sure it would be a positive experience. Two or three students could be asked to listen for and report the central idea in a reading rather than to do any reading. Parts could be read by everyone in unison. A soft-voiced person and a person with a strong voice could be asked to read a section together. People could be assigned paragraphs to read silently and to underline the central idea for sharing with the total class. People can stand up to read. A person who has difficulty sitting still for a long time could write key words, names, or ideas on the blackboard as they are mentioned by class members after a section has been read. You could add other ideas. The point is that even a simple activity like reading aloud can be sensitive to the diversity of student abilities, interests, and needs. The same principle can be applied to any other activity. The issue for teachers is to plan for ways in which specific students might engage in any activity, given the uniqueness of their abilities, interests, and needs.

If you would like to explore the usefulness of an activity for all the members of your class,

1. Choose a learning activity from one of the sessions in the teaching guide of the curricular resource you are using or that you have chosen for the session.————————

2. Is it an activity that interests you?————————————————————

3. What might hinder you from doing this activity well?————————————

——

4. If you do not have the time or ability to do it well, who could help you?——————

5. List the names of the members of your class below	In the column below, check whether you think each person would:		
	enjoy this activity	be able to do this activity	be challenged to grow (intellectually relationally, spiritually)

6. Review the list.
   a. Who might have serious problems with this activity?————————————

   ——

   ——

   b. How might you adapt the activity to make it interesting or appropriate to these persons?————————————————————————————————

   ——

   ——

A fourth way we create an environment of caring that has the potential to reveal God's love for those we teach is to *let our students know what we expect of them*. People feel at home in a place where they are comfortable. If they feel awkward, ill-at-ease, or out-of-place, they may conclude they are not welcome. When we have friends from out of town who are visiting us, we often give them a tour of our house, showing them where they will sleep and where their towels are hanging in the bathroom. This orients them to their new surroundings. It gives them a place in our home. They are now a part of our family. At some point we also outline our suggestions for their visit, describing what we might see and do, our schedule, and our thoughts about meals. We ask if these plans meet their approval. If they have any problems with the plans or had some other expectations for our visit, we then negotiate them. This gives us all a picture of what to expect during their stay. We can all relax now and enjoy ourselves. Our guests do not have to wonder about how to organize their visit, about what clothes to wear, or about how they will get around town. Instead, they can enter fully into the role of being a guest-family member. These familiar activities are a part of being hospitable.

Similar activities are crucial in the classroom. Students need to know what is expected of them and what they can expect of us. I usually call these expectations "ground rules" because they establish the boundaries within which we work. The Hebrews called the agreements establishing similar ground rules *covenants*. They establish our expectations of each other.

In a teaching-learning situation we have several kinds of expectations of student behavior. These have to do with the way students treat each other, the place we meet, and us. They include the way students relate to the content of our teaching and the way they participate in the learning activities planned for them. These expectations may have to do with being prepared for the class session and with the way students follow up class sessions at home, school, or work.

Of course, students also have expectations of us as teachers, of the content and experience in the classroom, of their peers, and of the importance of involvement in a religious education program for their lives. Often the expectations of teachers and students are in conflict with each other. That conflict is often the source of apathy and disruptive behavior among students and frustration and despair among teachers. These conflicts have to be negotiated if the atmosphere of the classroom is to be conducive to teaching and learning.

When expectations are clear, both students and teachers experience a sense of freedom. We can recognize the boundaries and are free to explore the territory inside them. I am reminded of one of my mother's firm rules when I was very small. We were not allowed to open any cupboard doors in the kitchen except the one with the pots and pans. But we had the freedom to open that one door. We could play with anything we found behind that door. We could use the contents of that cupboard in as many ways as we could imagine. In one sense, our behavior was constricted. In another, we had tremendous freedom.

By being clear about expectations we create an atmosphere of freedom. Freedom is a gift. It conveys trust and respect. It emphasizes mutuality and interdependence. Freedom is the premise of an open-ended future because it values the creativity, imagination, and spontaneity of persons within certain designated limits.

Clear expectations also create a disciplined environment. Discipline and freedom are closely related. I agree with Patrick Swazos Hinds, who described discipline as "dedication."[1] It is concerned with possibilities, not limits, and commitments, not restrictions. When we make our expectations known for our teaching, we make visible the possibilities for the quality of our relationships and for the significance of the content of our teaching for our futures. It is in our expectations that the possibilities of the kingdom of God become real to those we teach.

Discipline is not the same thing as control. Discipline makes use of limits to heighten our awareness of possibilities. We see this view of discipline at work in many games. In basketball, for example, the boundaries of the court limit the freedom of the players. At the same time, those boundaries challenge their creativity. If they are "disciplined," they develop several optional ways of moving the ball within the boundaries to accomplish the goal of making a basket. "Undisciplined" players are limited by their lack of optional plays.

In a similar fashion, the dedication of teachers and students to their task opens up a range of possibilities for their efforts. They develop increasingly useful skills for Bible study. They see the relationship between the gospel and daily life with increasing clarity. They experience the excitement of a deepening faith. Control functions differently. It makes use of limits to reduce options. For example, when a teacher faces the conflict between some people who want to learn and others who want to have fun, he or she is forced to limit the expectations of one of those groups. An option has been eliminated. When some people engage in destructive behavior, we are also often forced to establish limits. Whenever we do establish such limits, our actions should help clarify the ground rules for a group or class. Those limits clarify the boundaries within which the group functions. At that point limits may provide the basis for renewed commitment to the task—the first step in a disciplined life or group.

Although we usually attempt to clarify expectations of a class or a unit of study in the beginning, they must often be renegotiated:

1. when an event reveals an expectation we had not previously acknowledged. (We become aware of such expectations when something catches us unprepared or when we are disappointed, frustrated, or angry with the attitudes or actions of someone.)

2. when we become aware of the unstated expectations of students in their resistance or withdrawal from an activity.

3. when we become aware that the intellectual, spiritual, emotional, or physical growth of persons means that we can now expect more of them than we could previously.

4. when we become aware of tensions between the expectations experienced in the class we teach and those from the congregation or parish, the denomination, or the larger community in which people live.

5. when the commitment level of members in a class to each other intensifies and the group begins to assume increasing responsibility for the quality and character of its common life. The renegotiation of ground rules should be a sign of growth in us and those we teach. It can be evidence of an increasing openness to the will and work of God in our midst.

The Ministry of the Volunteer Teacher

If you would like to explore the expectations at work in your class, complete the following questions:

1. When you are well-prepared to teach, what expectations of yourself have you met?

_____

_____

_____

1. What do your students consider to be a good class session?

_____

_____

_____

2. What kind of preparation do you expect of those you teach?

_____

_____

_____

2. What do your students expect to do to prepare for a class session?

_____

_____

_____

3. What attitudes and behaviors do you expect of yourself?

_____

_____

_____

3. What attitudes and behaviors do members of your class expect of you?

_____

_____

_____

4. What attitudes and behaviors do you expect of those you teach?

_____

_____

_____

4. What attitudes and behaviors do the members of your class expect of themselves?

_____

_____

_____

5. What attitudes and behaviors will you not tolerate in yourself or in those you teach?

_____

_____

_____

5. What attitudes and behaviors will class members not tolerate in you or in themselves?

_____

_____

_____

6. Are any of your responses inconsistent with your understanding of the behavior we should expect in a Christian community?_____

_____

_____

_____

7. Are there conflicts between any of the responses in the two columns?_____

_____

_____

_____

8. If so, how might you clarify and negotiate those conflicts with those you teach so that you share common expectations for the class sessions?

_____

_____

_____

_____

_____

_____

CHAPTER 7

The Task of Creating a Caring Community

I am now teaching an adult Sunday school class that has been meeting for more than thirty years. It is an exciting class to teach. Discussions are lively, especially since there is a wide range of views on many topics. Class members are, for the most part, ready for the session. Most read the "lesson." The class continues to attract new members. And members seem to enjoy and care for each other deeply. In some respects it is not a homogeneous group. There is probably a twenty to twenty-five year age range. Some have children in grade school. Others have grandchildren in college. Some are married and some are single. Some lean to the political and theological right. Others lean to the political and theological left. Most find themselves sharing the values and ideals of a fairly large middle ground. Some have family ties in this community that go back generations and others are newcomers. What has held this group of people together for so many years?

As I have become familiar with the life of this class, I have discovered several things that its members do consistently. They freely share with each other reports of significant events in their lives. Currently many of these events have had to do with the birth and stories of grandchildren. Pictures are passed around, and anecdotes are shared. They call people who visit the worship services and invite them to the class. Many people arrive early so they can talk to each other. If newcomers enter the room someone immediately greets them and begins to introduce them to others present. If a crisis occurs in anyone's life, a response is organized. If appropriate, food is "collected." Reports of visits are shared. Every six weeks or so, the class has a covered-dish or potluck dinner together at someone's home. They contribute funds each week to respond to specific human needs in the church, in the city, and around the world. These consistent actions make up part of the ritual life of this class. In its simplest form, a ritual is an action that, through repetition, we begin to associate with certain events or situations. In its repetition the action becomes increasingly formal, even ceremonial. A birthday party does not feel complete, for example, until the guests have sung "Happy Birthday." A worship service feels unfinished for most of us if there is no sermon. This class I teach does not begin until the president has made the announcements and people have shared significant events. My day has not properly begun if I have not first had a chance to read the newspaper. These familiar, repeated, and expected actions are rituals. They mark the rhythmic movement of each day with greater clarity and meaning than the sweep of the hands of a clock. We move from the rituals of getting up to the rituals of breakfast to the rituals of leaving for work or school to the rituals of our jobs or our classrooms and so on through the day to the rituals of going to bed. So each class has its rituals too. Indeed, by the third meeting of a group many of those rituals are already in place. These repeated patterns of getting started, sharing concerns, worshiping, and carrying on a discussion pace our sessions together. They contribute as much to the sense of being at home as the furniture in the room. We count on having the chairs in place, and we count on certain things happening.

Many rituals may contribute to a caring environment when they bind us together and intensify our sense of being connected to each other. They can reinforce our sense of mutuality and concern for each other. In the class I teach, for example, the time we spend talking to each other before our discussion begins, the sharing of pictures of grandchildren, and the potluck suppers heighten our sense of being at-one with each other. In this and many other groups the hugs and handshakes demonstrate in a concrete way the ties that bind persons to each other. Similarly, the holding of hands during a closing prayer or the singing of a favorite song dramatizes the unity of a group's experience—another way of communicating God's care.

Some rituals sustain us through the rough times of crisis. Their familiarity supports us when we are lonely and hurting. I think of the flowers and cards that brighten hospital rooms and the food which people bring so we do not have to think about running to the store or preparing meals. I am reminded of the prayers and the soothing words of favorite scripture passages. Such rituals do not have to be somber. In our family we still laugh at the memory of the many plates of brownies brought to our house during a time of personal crisis. And we cherish the humor of the get-well cards that both brighten our day and convey concern. These rituals are important to us because they make it possible for us to express our feelings beyond our words.

Other rituals energize us for new challenges—also a sign of God's care. Promotions at school and work are familiar illustrations. So are the rituals that surround joining a congregation, parish, or class, that sanction the selection of new leaders and officers for a group, or that celebrate new tasks and responsibilities related to our sense of purpose in life. Obviously, rituals like those involved in an election become a formal part of the life of organizations and groups. Others are less obvious. For example, I am intrigued by the heightened interest that usually accompanies the beginning of a new study unit in many adult classes. Special statements announce the new unit. Attendance increases. All make sure they have the books. A greater proportion of the class reads the first chapter or section. Group members talk of their high expectations for the study. This pattern of behavior occurs with each new unit and rekindles our excitement in the group's commitment to engage in some study program. We are presented with a new opportunity, a new challenge.

As teachers, we cannot escape the fact that our classes will have a rich ritual life. We can help shape, however, the content of those rituals. We may refuse to perpetrate insensitive or unhelpful rituals. We may also introduce or reinforce rituals that help reveal our common commitment to be the body of Christ.

These rituals

1. heighten our awareness that "we are one in the Spirit" and that this oneness is revealed in the quality of our care for each other.
2. give us a sense of purposeful continuity over the months and years.
3. sustain us in times of stress and crisis when our personal strength and resources seem to be inadequate.
4. mobilize us for specific actions of service to God and our neighbor in study, worship, and mission.

Rituals that create bonds of mutuality and care can be either simple or elaborate. They can be brief or take a long period of time. They can be a structured part of a teaching plan or they can be spontaneous. They share some common features as actions that gather us into the bonding work of the Holy Spirit.

In any ritual

1. *A situation or event is announced.* This action focuses the group's attention upon the person(s) involved. It gives everyone the same information. It heightens the group's expectations.

2. *The group responds to the announcement.* This response may include a corporate act like singing "Happy Birthday" and individual actions as in the giving of gifts or sending of cards. It may involve a decision to send a card, flowers, or food, to request more information, or to organize a response.

3. *A blessing is given.* This action makes clear that those involved in the ritual recognize and affirm God's presence as the source of the power that heals, renews, and strengthens us for the demands and challenges of our situation. A blessing may take many forms—a benediction, a hymn, a prayer, or a statement anticipating the future. It may be offered by one person or the whole group. It often uses religious language, but it often uses common words that have the potential to convey religious meanings.

4. *Those involved in the situation or event make a response.* At its simplest level, a person may express words of appreciation to the group for their love or concern. They may lead the group in a prayer of thanksgiving. They may share their hopes and dreams for the future. They may offer a gift to the group or to a project important to the group as a sign of their gratefulness. For example, in my childhood church, people of all ages contributed a penny for each year they had lived to the congregation's mission fund on their birthdays.

All four actions need to be present. If any is missing, the ritual is often experienced as incomplete. The potential of the ritual to embody the care of class members is limited. Those involved may leave with a sense of disappointment, frustration, and sometimes rejection. It is not a rational feeling. It is, instead, the gnawing sensation that something is not quite right. For the most part, we have learned to tolerate these feelings. But their presence lowers our expectation of that group's ability to reflect the love and concern we associate with those who are gathered in the name of Christ.

Another common experience also diminishes the effectiveness of rituals to nurture our common life as the people of God. When all members of a group are not equally included in a ritual activity, the care of the group is distributed unevenly. The pain of a forgotten birthday or an ignored illness, for example, is not easy to forget if a class regularly recognizes those events. It can cause some people to drop out of class and others to believe that they are less important to the group. Unless a ritual is created with the approval of the whole class for a special occasion, all members should be honored in the common ritual activities of the group.

There are many kinds of rituals—so many, in fact, that no class or group can make use of them all.

1. *Some are related to our growth as persons.* These rituals recognize and celebrate the changes we experience with the passage of time. Birthdays, for example, mark the relentless march of the years revealed in the processes of maturation and aging. Baptism, first communion, conversion, confirmation, and the events that renew those experiences celebrate our spiritual growth. Starting school, promotions, graduation,

first and new jobs, marriage, changes in vocation, birth of children, and retirement provide occasions for rituals of social growth.

2. Other rituals provide structures for *coping with the crises of our lives:* illness, job loss, divorce, death, and personal misfortunes of one kind or another. They sustain us in the midst of our grief, pain, and anger. They also make it possible for others to shoulder some of the burden we are carrying. We have often developed useful rituals to convey our concern for those who are sick or bereaved. It is my hunch, however, that few groups have yet established rituals that reveal God's love to those caught up in divorce proceedings, job loss, school failure, or some socially unacceptable behavior such as having a child arrested for dealing drugs in school or being the child arrested. Perhaps the real test of the quality of the care of a group occurs when the group must respond to a member in one of those situations.

3. Another set of rituals *builds and reinforces a sense of group identity and mutuality.* Rituals celebrating the commitment of persons joining the group and the contribution of those who are moving away or leaving the group belong to this category. So do the activities that follow up on absentees, and the special events that provide a different setting for deepening relationships.

4. One other set of rituals *helps organize the corporate life of the class or group.* These rituals are usually evident in the way officers and leaders are chosen and honored. They are also located in the activities that extend the class or group's work beyond itself, in service to others or as a part of larger outreach concerns of the congregation or parish. For example, I think of some classes of children who have adopted shut-ins as their special friends. They developed certain ritual expectations around the plans, visits, and gifts to be taken to these older friends. This ritual activity provides the children with an opportunity to participate in Christ's ministry to others.

All four kinds of rituals are appropriate with all ages. The words or actions used may vary from age group to age group. But it is obvious that everyone has birthdays. Every class has persons who are absent from time to time. The social circumstances of all people do change, and those changes need to be acknowledged, and the people involved need to experience the bond of community in their new situation. The recent widow in a class of couples, for example, feels out of place until that class finds a way to make her comfortable with them in her new role. The person who loses a job feels out of place in a class in which everyone else seems to be securely employed until the class makes clear his or her acceptability. The examples vary, but children and teenagers also experience the loneliness in familiar groups caused by changes in their lives until the group makes tangible the message that they are still valued. Even rituals having to do with the organizational life of a class are relevant to groups of young children. They also have their "helpers" who provide the most basic of leadership tasks. Their efforts need to be recognized and affirmed as much as the officers of a youth group or adult class.

These common experiences are not ordinary. We have intense feelings about their significance in our lives. The ritual makes it possible for us to share their meanings with others, to celebrate those things which delight us, and to discover the resources to live through those things that are painful. These events take on religious significance if the rituals dramatize the compassion, concern, and joy of God as the source of their meaning for us. And the rituals become, then, an important way of expressing God's love and care for us.

The Ministry of the Volunteer Teacher

If you would like to become aware of some of the rituals in your class,

1. Respond to the questions listed in each column:

Ritual Event	Who usually announces the event? What do they usually say?	What is the typical response of the group to the announcement?	Who offers a "blessing" for the person(s) involved? What do they usually say or do?	Are there opportunities for people to respond to this ritual action?
Birthdays				
Greeting visitors				
Saying goodby and thank you to people who are moving away				
Illness; personal crises (divorce, death, etc.); responding to absentees				
Celebrating events of spiritual growth				
Expressing appreciation to people for leader-ship or special contributions				
Helping persons or groups out-side the class				
Other				

2. Which rituals most effectively express care for persons?

3. Which rituals are less helpful in expressing care for persons?

4. What suggestions do you have to fill in the gaps or to increase the effectiveness of any of these rituals?

5. Are there rituals that should be introduced to the class to care for group members more effectively?

CHAPTER 8

The Task of Being a Caregiver

Several years ago a pastor friend told me about an unusual teacher of a Sunday school class for older children. Among the members of the class was a child with a terminal illness. When the doctor said the child would no longer be able to leave her house, the teacher, after a conversation with the child's parents, asked the rest of the class if they would like their sessions to meet at the child's home. The class endorsed the suggestion. They organized a carpool to travel to and from the child's home, where they met until death claimed her life. This teacher symbolizes for me one other way that we as teachers help create a caring environment for those we teach. She cared for her students. She made it possible for a very sick child to be with friends in a learning situation. That act revealed the teacher's sense of hope. She involved children in a natural way in surrounding that child with their own lively forms of concern and compassion. She conveyed by her action that death was not to be feared but challenged and that sick people were not to be pitied but gathered up into vital living.

For all of us Jesus is the master teacher. Our relationship to him is as the branches to the vine. It is he who first taught that which we seek to teach. It is his life that we attempt to emulate. It is in his dependence upon God that we are strengthened to "bear fruit" or to be agents of God's reconciling love.

In our teaching, our own relationship to Jesus Christ is most evident when those we teach are able to see Christ through us in the way we care for them and others. In other words, our actions do not bring attention to ourselves, but instead they honor the one we serve. They reveal Christ at work in and through us. In our own faithfulness, Christ is present for those we teach.

This experience in our teaching does not come by attending to our own religious behavior as much as it comes in the giving of ourselves for another. Perhaps the most powerful illustration of this fact is found in the Gospel of Matthew: Jesus declares that those who feed the hungry, give drink to the thirsty, clothe the naked, comfort the sick, and visit the imprisoned will serve him and, in the process, meet him. Jesus, of course, referred to those deprived of basic life-sustaining resources. Many of us teach persons whose basic needs are not being met. We would be teaching even more of these persons if our congregations and parishes were known by their acceptance of those who suffer as brothers and sisters in Christ. In the teaching relationship, however, we also encounter those who are hungry for meaning and purpose, thirsty for justice, vulnerable because of their ignorance, weak due to their doubts, and imprisoned by shackles of prejudice and bigotry. Our work as teachers brings us face-to-face with the deepest expressions of human pain and suffering taken on by the Christ, if we but have the eyes to see it and the ears to hear it. That was the gift of the teacher I have just described. She could see beyond the surface realities of sickness, loneliness, and death to the possibilities for "life," not only in the sick child in her class but in each person she taught.

It is not easy to care for others—at least at the points of their deepest needs. It may take more time and energy than we planned to give. I am sure that this teacher had not expected to be organizing car pools, leaving home earlier on Sunday mornings, or making sure that the activities she had chosen could work in a home with a child growing weaker and weaker.

Caring for others may lead us into places we had not expected to be. I think of the church group who found themselves visiting a church member's son in prison or of the teacher calling on a family in a section of town she feared because of the stories she had heard about the lack of safety there.

Caring for others may confront us with some of our own deepest fears and anxieties. Sickness and death confront us with a finitude we often seek to ignore. Poverty makes us face up to the inequities and injustice of human experience. The doubts and ignorance of others may reveal the superficiality and shallowness of our own faith. An abused child or a battered spouse may challenge our fear of becoming involved. And so the list could go on. It is not always easy to care for those we teach in the name of Jesus Christ. Yet probably nothing transforms the atmosphere of a teaching-learning event more than the care a teacher has for his or her students. Much as a candle lights up a whole room, a faithful person's actions create an environment of grace by revealing the source of that grace in the midst of those in need.

Practicing the Presence of God

To become a caregiver involves practice. The task is similar to the exercise of "practicing the presence of God" in the literature on spirituality. This phrase simply means that we discover the presence of God by practicing behaviors based on the assumption that we are in the presence of God. It is like a pianist who mentally hears how a musical phrase should sound and repeats it over and over in practice sessions until the actual sound matches it. In practicing the care of God, I would like to suggest three different exercises. Each has the potential of enhancing our sensitivity to the tasks of being a caregiver.

As teachers we are more than the funnel for transferring information, values, and ways of behaving from a curricular resource book to a child, teen, or adult. In one sense at least, Marshall MacLuhan was right. The medium, that is, the teacher, is in an important way the message. We reveal the power of the gospel in our lives. Its value to students is evident in its credibility to us. This is not an unfamiliar idea. As I look back on my own experience in both church and school, the teachers who most influenced me were those who seemed to be totally caught up in their subject matter. Their excitement with chemistry, English literature, or the Old Testament stories of Hebrew faith caught my attention, aroused my curiosity, and challenged me to take seriously the methods of study, values, and content of their courses. It is no less true of the Christian teacher whose own faithfulness best reveals the meaning of being a disciple of Christ.

This task may seem awesome. Most volunteer teachers are not Bible scholars, theologians, or psychologists trained in the subtleties of human nature. But we should not be overwhelmed by the challenge. Jesus turned, for the most part, to people whose potential was to be found in their faithfulness. The issue was not how much they knew, but to what extent they were disciples or students of the one who called them. That same challenge is ours.

That challenge is most obviously found in the value we place on what we teach. Through our teaching we seek to make certain goals for the Christian life and the content of the Christian experience credible to our students. The issue for us has to do with the credibility of those goals and experiences for our own lives. If the subject of our teaching speaks to us, we may witness to its power in and through our teaching. Consequently, one way to practice being a caregiver is to explore the claim of the objectives in our teaching plans for our own faith and lives.

Most of us use some kind of curricular resource. It may be a specially prepared resource. For most of us, it will have been approved for use in congregations or parishes of our denomination. It may be a designated chapter or two from a book of the Bible we are studying. This printed material is our starting point. From it we develop a plan for our teaching. But first, we need to explore its message for ourselves. If we do not sense its meaning for us, should we expect those we teach to take it seriously?

Over the years I have discovered that the following tasks help me discover implications for my own life in the resources from which I teach. They also help prevent me from teaching a resource "for the good of the children, teenagers, or adults" in my class as if my own faithfulness and goodness were somehow superior to theirs. You may choose to modify, add to, or drop some of the questions. The form is not as important as the exercise of being claimed by the content of what we teach.

1. Read all the material related to the topic or unit of study to be used with your class so that you have an overview of the issues, ideas, and experiences involved and the way they are developed by the author.

2. In a sentence or two describe why it is important to the church for the members of your class to engage in this study.

3. In a sentence or two describe why it is important to you personally to teach this unit.

4. If you were to take the themes in this unit seriously for your own faith and life, what differences would they make in your own relationship to God?

In the way you serve your neighbor?

In the way you teach your class?

To Pray for Those We Teach

In one sense, prayer is the activity of relating ourselves to God in such a way that we begin to see the world around us from God's perspective. It is the act of letting go of our own preconceptions, biases, and prejudices. John and Adrienne Carr have discussed this dimension of prayer in the *Experiment of Practical Christianity* (Nashville: Discipleship Resources, 1986), a resource for groups exploring what it means to live as Christians in today's world. In an exercise called "Seeing People Real," the participants are led into the practice of intercessory prayer for the members of their group. Groups evaluating this exercise consistently gave it high marks. It helped group members become better acquainted, feel closer, and deepen their concern for each other.

Intercessory prayer is the act of walking the second mile with another person. It is, in the words of the Native American saying, to walk in the moccasins of another. These familiar words point to the fact that when we lift up the name of someone in prayer we step into his or her world. We suspend judgment to let the pieces of the puzzle of that person's life begin to fall into place. We open ourselves to serve as channels of gospel or good news for this person. In the process we may discover a clue to things we might say and do as agents of God's love.

I remember a boy in a junior high class I taught several years back. He was one of the most disruptive persons I have ever taught. The class was large and active. His behavior only made a bad teaching situation worse. His actions were not malicious or destructive, just disruptive. His hyperactivity was part of the problem. He had an attention span of no more than forty-five seconds under normal conditions. We timed his attention span. We analyzed his behavior with categories from psychology. We asked if he had had proper medical attention. But it was not until we began "to lift his name in prayer" that we began to see him "real."

Our new insights did not change psychological and medical diagnoses. But they did help us to see that our attitudes contributed to his "problem." We judged him by our standards, not God's. All our efforts had been directed at controlling his behavior to make the classroom situation easier for us. Consequently, he was like a pressure cooker—almost always ready to let off steam. No one, moreover, had helped him to discover legitimate outlets for these explosive moments. So we took a walk together—a second-mile walk to talk about his experience, given these behaviors. We concluded that conversation with a simple decision. Whenever he felt he could no longer contain his emotions, he would quietly leave the room, go outside, and run around the building. No loitering would be acceptable, and church school officers were informed of our agreement. For two or three weeks he seemed to be out of class more than he was in, but our sessions were not being disrupted. It was not long, however, before the number of his laps around the church building began to decrease. His behavior was never perfect, but his participation increased in helpful ways when we began to look at his life from a larger vantage point.

To pray for others is not a complicated task, but it takes time. We may find it helpful to set aside a quiet time, or we may discover that we can pray while we are washing dishes, mowing the lawn, or driving to work—in other words, during a routine job. We may choose to spend a little time each week on each person in the class, or we may spread their names out over a month or a quarter. We may choose to pray in silence, or we may write down any thoughts that occur while in the spirit of prayer. Those are the mechanics of intercessory prayer. There is nothing mysterious about the act of intercessory prayer. It simply involves choosing a time, a place, and an approach that seems appropriate to us.

The Ministry of the Volunteer Teacher

To begin the discipline of intercessory prayer several questions may help guide your meditations on viewing another person from God's perspective:

A. What is the person's name?

B. What has he or she said and done that I can recall? In other words, can I see him or her with some of the vividness that God can?

C. What are the "gifts" he or she brings to our class? How are these gifts received by us? How have we nurtured those gifts? How have we refused them?

D. Is there any pain in this person's life? What causes it? What about joy? Where is it located?

E. What are my feelings about this person? How have I treated him or her? In what ways do my words and actions convey God's care for him or her?

F. What would be "good news" to this person?

G. Is there any way for our class to be an agent of good news for him or her? Is there anything I might say or do to be an agent of good news?

To Stay Out of God's Way

Remember when Jesus sent the seventy-two men out to preach, teach, and heal? They returned from their mission filled with wonder at what they had been able to do when they spoke in Jesus' name. The first line in Carolyn M. Noel's hymn, "At the name of Jesus every knee shall bow," celebrates the awe and wonder Paul experienced when proclaiming the reconciling love of Jesus Christ. Faithful men and women through the ages have similarly pondered the mystery of the effect of their ministries in the lives of people. When we respond to the call to extend the mission of Christ to others, we become the instruments of his work and will. We become the hands, feet, and voice of the one who sent us. In our case, the field of our effort is the classroom or some other place where people gather to learn.

As volunteer teachers we encounter the ignorance that perpetuates the divisiveness and cruelty of obstinate national, ethnic, cultural, and religious pride. We contend with the confusion in values and ideals of people searching for some sign of hope, purpose, and meaning in life. We listen to the stories of the powerlessness of women, children, and men who can find no way out of the traps of contemporary social structures and systems. We see the idolatry of people casting about for something to which they might commit themselves. And we dare to speak in Jesus' name.

As we teach we may notice changes taking place in the lives of some people. Occasionally a person's life may be radically transformed through something we did or said. Perhaps we introduced an activity that culminated in a heightened sense of solidarity and clarity of common purpose among the members of the group we teach. But these changes are not the consequences of our own efforts, as important as these efforts are. These changes are due to the power of God at work in and through us. They occur as we open ourselves to the possibility of being agents of God's grace through teaching. They are occasional signs of our own trust and devotion.

This observation leads me to one other way that we may be a caregiver in and through our teaching. It involves getting out of the way when a person or group begins to respond to God's call. Perhaps the example of the old priest Eli is helpful here. As you recall the story, Samuel had spent some time "serving the Lord under the direction of Eli" (I Samuel 3:1 TEV). He had undoubtedly listened to the many stories Eli told of God's efforts to protect and save the Hebrew people. He had learned how to be helpful to Eli in his priestly duties. The implication of the story is that Samuel had been a willing student and that Eli had been a sensitive and effective teacher. Yet in the dark of the night when God called his name, Samuel thought the voice was Eli's. His primary loyalty as a student belonged to Eli. He did not yet recognize the source of the power in Eli's teaching. But Eli did. He finally urged Samuel to return to bed and when he next heard his name to answer, "Speak, Lord, your servant is listening" (I Samuel 3:9 TEV). Eli got out of the way. He had done his job.

In one sense we are describing the limitations of the teacher's role. Teachers provide background information. They create experiences to prepare persons for moments of insight that might illuminate or give meaning to an event or to their lives. They encourage students. They challenge and discipline them. But teachers cannot learn for a student. They cannot answer for a student when that student directly confronts some sign of God's creative and reconciling power. Yet this moment is a crucial one for the teacher as it is for the student.

In the first phase, the teacher helps students to recognize the signs of God's work among them. The situation is much like a medical school professor describing in class the symptoms of a disease. The students now have relevant information. They know about the disease. It is not, however, until the students are shown a patient with the disease that the vividness of its reality is imprinted on their memories. They "see" it for the first time. They "hear" the description given in the classroom with understanding that's only available through experience. The professor is now an outsider to the student's learning.

As teachers we find ourselves similarly involved in pointing out to our students the work and presence of God in their midst and in the world around them. It may occur in helping those we teach recognize or "see" that certain attitudes and actions are consistent with the character and will of God:

- when a self-centered child shares a toy without being told to do so.
- when the members of a class experience a rare moment of intimacy revealing their openness to transcendent power at work in their midst.
- when two people with contrary views on issues discover truths in each other's position.
- when a political leader acts to bring relief to the oppressed.

It may occur in helping those we teach recognize or "see" the presence of a transforming power in the midst of their daily experiences and relationships:

- when persons discover a sense of freedom in the midst of the routines of their lives.
- when someone connects an insight from a passage of scripture to a problem at school or work.
- when someone realizes that in spite of feeling quite unacceptable, God's love is unconditional. The task is not to prove that we can be acceptable, but that we have already been accepted.
- when someone comes to terms with his or her own involvement in the injustices of the world and determines to participate in activities to alleviate pain and suffering.

In the second phase, the teacher's task is to help students name the source of these experiences. To name something is to give it power in our lives. To name something means that we accept its claim on our lives. It is the basis for the mutuality of relationships. It is a sign of our willingness to be open to the possibilities that may develop due to that relationship. It is the impetus to our own responsiveness to God's initiative. With Samuel we can acknowledge who calls us, "Lord, I am listening." To help students recognize and name their encounters with the

Holy is one of the most powerful expressions of caregiving possible. It reveals our own relationship to the source of God's grace. Even more, it shifts our students' attention from us to the one who sustains us.

The task is often a subtle one. It is often directed beyond the tangible objects available directly to our senses of sight, touch, hearing, and smell. This is the point Jesus made repeatedly to those he healed: "Your faith has made you well." Jesus saw the trust those people placed in God's ability to heal through him. As teachers we point to those moments when the healing, transforming, creating, renewing, and reconciling work of God is evident in the trustful responsiveness of those we teach. It is evident when a teacher of young children says, "I saw God at work today in this room. I saw God's love when Marjorie shared her crayons with Johnny. I saw God's love when Peter told Steven he was sorry he had hit him. I saw God's love when Bobby hugged Mrs. Smith. Where did you see God's love?" God's love was evident in those actions revealing the trust of these children to risk themselves with another, to reach out, and to be vulnerable. It is in such commonplace events, just as it is in the common action of sharing bread and wine, that we risk the possibility of encountering the presence of God. To help those we teach "see" the work of God or to "hear" the voice of God in those events means that we see our teaching as a means to introduce persons to the source of the care that nurtures, inspires, and sustains us all. In those moments of recognition and response to God's grace on the part of those we teach, we may find ourselves sharing the awe and wonder of the seventy-two disciples. It is then that we celebrate being teachers, agents of God's love committed to the tasks of building up the body of Christ for the purposes of praising God and serving our neighbors.

PART IV

The Work of the Volunteer Teacher: To Mediate Good News from Our Past for Our Future

Introduction

We have just been comparing our work as teachers to that of a host or hostess. Other metaphors also come to mind as I think of the responsibilities connected with teaching. Among them is that of the tour guide. Like the tour guide, the teacher leads people into an adventure. Both point to the possibility of new experiences. Each helps people to see new sights, to think new thoughts, to try something strange and different. Each challenges old ways of seeing and acting, provides guidelines, and prepares for emergencies. Both know that their words and actions may lead some people to make decisions that could radically alter their lives.

It is risky—even audacious—to take a group of people who have never ridden a horse or hiked more than two or three miles to the bottom of the Grand Canyon. It is risky because the tour guide has no way of knowing what an inexperienced rider or hiker might do—even with careful preparation. Yet tour guides lead hundreds of such people down those steep, winding, hot, and dry trails to the Colorado River far below year after year.

To introduce to a group of people the mysteries of the Bible, the history of the church, a critique of contemporary events in the light of the gospel, or the skills of empathetic listening or missional outreach is also a risky and audacious task. The teacher has no way of knowing what people will do when they are seized by the power of a story, or when a passage of scripture reveals a vision or purpose for their lives, or when they begin to use the skills of charity they learned in the "safe" environment of some classroom or group in the church.

And yet, tour guides and teachers engage in their work with the hope that the lives of people will be changed through the experience. For teachers in the church, as we have already said, that hope undergirds the faith that their efforts will contribute to the building up of the church so that all might glorify God and respond with compassion to the needs of their neighbors. It is this future in which peace, love, and justice symbolize the common bond of our obedience to God that commands the attention of the teacher.

That future does not just happen. Perhaps a comparison with the tour guide is again helpful. Guides leading a group to the bottom of the Grand Canyon, to the top of a mountain, or even on a tour of landmarks in a city must be prepared. They must be familiar with the route. They must have made arrangements for whatever meals are involved. They need to have first-aid skills and be attuned to the safety hazards of the trip. They need some skills in organizing a group of people to do whatever needs to be done for the common good. They need to understand and respect the environment and the inhabitants of the territory through which they travel. We could extend the list. These "requirements of the job," however, may illustrate the necessity for planning any venture.

59

We need to point out before going any further that in our highly organized world, few tour guides do all this planning themselves. Most receive help from people who have studied what is needed for a venture and have developed a basic plan for all tour guides. Similarly, the curriculum resources produced by church publishing houses provide a basic plan for teachers in the church. But tour guides and teachers who follow these basic plans may well be unable to do their tasks in special situations if they themselves do not know how to plan. A teacher who inherits a class of "poor" readers simply cannot use a plan designed for "good" readers "as is." A person who teaches people from a wide variety of cultural or socio-economic backgrounds or with a wide range of physical or intellectual abilities often finds that these basic plans are insensitive to differences in people. A teacher who discovers just before a class session begins that a member of the class has been severely injured in an automobile accident may well have to alter his or her plans on the spot. Other unexpected circumstances can also disrupt our expectations for our teaching. For these reasons, it is my belief that all teachers—even those who use prescribed plans—need to know the basic elements in planning for teaching.

The process for planning a teaching session or unit is evident in a series of questions which must always be answered. Again the similarity between the teacher and the tour guide becomes apparent. Both must deal with these questions.

1. Who will be a part of this venture?
2. Why do they want to go on this venture? (Because they have always done it? Because their parents require it? Because they desire to know what it means to live the new life in Christ? Because everybody else is going? etc.)
3. Where are they going? (In other words, what is the destination or goal of this venture?)
4. What do they need to know to get the most out of this experience and to reach their destination?
5. By what means will they move toward their destination?
6. What do they need to take with them?
7. What arrangements need to be made to ensure that they can concentrate upon the venture?

We ask these questions to make sure that we are ready for the venture. Planning has to do with our readiness for an experience or event. If we do not have clarity about why we are going someplace, we run the risk of being disappointed with our destination. The venture may prove to be boring or unrelated to our concerns. If we have not chosen appropriate methods to reach our goals, we often experience frustration. If we do not have the resources and supplies we need, we may end up as the foolish virgins did in the parable told by Jesus—standing outside locked doors listening to the sounds of celebration. Planning is crucial to the venture of teaching. It provides the background work necessary for being ready to teach.

In the pages that follow we will examine in more detail these various questions.

CHAPTER 9

Students and Teachers: The "Who" in Teaching

One of the most obvious influences on the content and quality of an educational experience is who is in the class—the students. Anyone who has taught knows this to be true. The personalities, extent of family support, interests and abilities of its members all affect the way a group behaves, what it values, and how it approaches a teaching-learning event.

It does not take long before we begin to discover the corporate personality of the group we teach. I think of one class of third graders in a parish I once served. The children would "burst" into the room; they rarely walked. Teachers quickly realized that this group would be a lively and energetic one. Soon other characteristics became evident. The class was dominated by a large group of boys. They were intelligent, athletic, and close friends. A little background information would reveal they all came from families who were active in the church and who valued a strong religious education program. Attendance would be almost guaranteed. But so would chaos in the classroom if they were not challenged and interested. Teachers who had grown accustomed to the quiet agreeableness of the previous third-grade class soon discovered that last year's plans and approaches did not work well with this group.

These differences are evident not only from one group or class to another, but are found within each group in the diversity of personalities, commitments, interests, needs, and abilities we discussed earlier. The differences we encounter in those we teach affect the way we prepare for our teaching. The teachers in the third-grade class I just described, for example, had something planned for each person as soon as he or she arrived to make sure that the attention and energy of each child was directed immediately toward the goals of the class session. The pacing of the class activities tended to be faster than the year before and the activities themselves involved considerable student initiative.

We have already discussed ways to account for the diversity of interests, needs, abilities, and experiences among class members. Attention to those differences does influence our plans. We did not describe, however, the impact of the gifts of those we teach on the conduct of a class session. I am reminded of a talented four-year-old boy. He was often the ringleader in group play. He seemed to notice almost immediately if a child was not participating and would try to include that child in some way. His teacher quickly discovered that her effectiveness depended, in part, upon using his leadership skills. Although she was the teacher, her teaching influence depended in part upon his ability or gift to lead his peers into a learning activity.

I am also reminded of a fifth-grade girl who read the entire curricular resource the week after receiving it. She would sometimes add to her knowledge of the topic by further reading in the encyclopedia and other resource books. She sometimes ended up leading a discussion in the class because her own investigation of a topic was more thorough than the teacher's had been. And I am reminded of my own experience as a young pastor encountering an engineer in the congregation who had read extensively in the writings of such famous theologians as Paul Tillich, Reinhold Niebuhr, and Karl Barth. In both these instances, a "student" may well have been "teaching" the "teacher."

The gifts and experience of those we teach, in other words, may alter the traditional way of viewing the teacher as "the one who knows" and the student as "the one who is to learn what the teacher knows." This view may be appropriate in some situations, but all too often it has immobilized the volunteer teacher. It has led many people to refuse to teach because they "do not know enough." And it has led others to conclude that their "teaching" is not as important as the quality of their relationships with their students. Both responses demean the role of the teacher and diminish the importance of teaching to the mission of the church.

I would like us to rethink the relationship of the teacher both to students and to the content of teaching. In the first place, we as teachers *are accountable for the conduct of the educational ministry in our congregation or parish*. I use the word *accountable* in the technical sense. We have been given a task. There comes a time when we must give an accounting for what we have done with the gift of our calling. Our situation is much like that of the three men in Jesus' parable of the talents. Each teacher has been entrusted with a part of the church's ministry of teaching. The question we must face has to do with the quality of our investment in that ministry.

We will not be judged by what our students learn. That is their responsibility. Just as with teachers of any age, we will face students with "closed minds" and "hardened hearts." We cannot force such persons to learn. We cannot make people into faithful disciples of Jesus Christ. Each student must decide to make use of our teaching.

Instead, we are responsible for our teaching. That is what we have been given. And it is what will be assessed. Among the questions we face as we consider the way we have treated our calling, the following seem to me to be especially important.

What did we do with our gift of teaching? With this question we are faced with our attitude toward both the gift of teaching we have accepted and the One who is the source of the gift. Did we hide the gift in superficial teaching? Did we use it to our own gain? Did we use it in such a way as to impede or hinder the learning of those we were supposed to teach? Did we use it to expand the knowledge and skills of those we teach? Did we teach as if our own authority superceded God's? Did we teach, resenting the demands that the gift—and God—seemed to place on us? Are we grateful for the gift and its challenges to us?

Has our teaching been faithful to the gospel? With this question we are faced with the extent to which we have been open to the leading of the Holy Spirit through our teaching. Have we allowed ourselves to be caught up in theological fads? Have we limited the gospel we teach to a particular doctrinal position? Have we confused the gospel we teach with the values held by our family, congregation, denomination, social class, or nation? Have we reduced our teaching to clever educational activities that keep people busy, but also may prevent them from encountering the gospel?

Has our teaching revealed the gospel? In this question we are faced with the consistency between our words, attitudes, and actions. Does the content of our teaching mean anything to us? Do our methods and relationships reinforce and support the content of our teaching? Do our students see the goal of our teaching reflected in our own lives?

We may be accountable but *we do not have to do all the teaching.* That is the second observation I would make about our relationship to those we teach. Perhaps a journey metaphor is helpful. When our children were young and we were planning our vacations, my wife and I were responsible for all parts of the trip. As our children grew, our plans also changed because our children could assume some of the tasks we had previously done. They could make the list of clothes and toys they would take and check their lists with us (the point of our responsibility). They could suggest activities for the family to include on our itinerary and test them with us for their appropriateness as to cost, time, and purpose. They soon took responsibility for packing their suitcases and later the car. Eventually they took their turns driving the car and planning side trips for the family. I foresee in the near future a time when they will be primarily responsible for a trip in which we will participate. Then the roles will be completely reversed. We will become students to their "teaching."

The process that took place in our family is typical for teachers who see in their students the future leadership of the community of faith. That is always the task of teachers. Repeatedly Jesus drew his disciples aside in an attempt to prepare them for the time when he would no longer be present. He gave them responsibilities to test and refine their knowledge, skills, and commitment toward that end. Similarly, we share leadership with the children, teenagers, and adults we teach. We provide opportunities for them to test their growth in knowledge, to develop their skills in communicating the gospel, and to discover the transforming power of God in the midst of their own efforts.

As I write these words, however, my memory is filled with incidents when teachers of all age groups asked persons to do something and then gave them no instructions and little support and allowed them to get away with less than their best efforts. The educational experience for everyone consequently was trivial. The gospel had been shortchanged. And the student was demeaned. When we ask children, teenagers, or adults to participate in the teaching of a session, our instructions must be clear regarding the task and the expected quality of their work. We must see that they have the necessary resources for their efforts and that they receive whatever training is essential to their own sense of self-esteem as a child of God.

Sharing leadership is a significant part of the planning process for teaching. It celebrates the diversity of gifts within a class or group. It reminds all of their involvement in the shaping of a future for the church. And it helps those of us who are the designated teachers from becoming immobilized by what we do not yet know. We find ourselves on a journey *with* those we teach.

The Ministry of the Volunteer Teacher

If you would like to improve the way you involve others in the leadership of your teaching, use the following guide:

1. Review the plans for your teaching session.

2. What tasks or parts of the plan might others do? / Who might do them? / What training or supervision might they need?

   A. _____ _____ _____

   _____ _____ _____

   _____ _____ _____

   B. _____ _____ _____

   _____ _____ _____

   _____ _____ _____

   C. _____ _____ _____

   _____ _____ _____

   _____ _____ _____

3. How much advance notice would each person need?

   _____

   _____

   _____

4. What resources might each person need?

   _____

   _____

   _____

5. Do you have the time to help all the people prepare for their parts in the session? If not, who might?

   _____

   _____

   _____

Objectives: The "Why" of Teaching

Although I do not intend to use the metaphor of a journey or trip with each of the elements in a teaching plan, it is particularly helpful when discussing the objectives that guide and shape our approaches to teaching.[1] Almost three years ago in a family gathering, it was unanimously agreed to celebrate my wife's parents' fiftieth wedding anniversary. Because we live about twenty-five hundred miles from their home in California, that family decision established the destination for our summer travels the year of the celebration. As we began to look forward to that trip, our own expectations began to expand. We decided to include a visit to my family in Oregon. We arranged our itinerary so that we could stay with good but rarely seen friends along the way. We planned for some sightseeing and relaxing as well. These expectations established our route of travel, our timetable, the kinds of things we did, and the preparations we made for the trip.

A similar pattern emerges from our planning for teaching. For example, a month from now the class I teach will begin a study of the life and work of Peter. That decision was made by the members of the class after a discussion of several options. Some comments in that discussion began to shape our expectations of this study. "What was Peter like as a person?" "I've always been fascinated by the relationship of the man to Jesus." "What happened to Peter after the resurrection appearances?" "Did he really found the church in Rome?" "I really don't know much about the man." These comments revealed that we were interested in more than a summary of Peter's life and ideas. They also began to point to an itinerary for the weeks ahead. They created an agenda for us. In educational language, they helped to clarify our objectives for our study. Every teaching plan begins with at least one objective, grounded in the expectations that the church and we bring to it.

These objectives establish a destination for our teaching and learning. The objective in our class will be to explore the life and faith of Peter. Each week we will meet to share in that venture. Each time we meet we will be guided by more specific objectives related to the topic or question at hand. In both instances, the objective identifies our task. It sets boundaries on our efforts. We will not be trying to explore everything in the New Testament or even to understand the life and work of all the disciples. It pulls us into the future. When we complete the study, we should be able to look back and identify our learnings—what we have seen, thought, heard, and done along the way.

An objective has a second function. *It identifies for those we teach what the church (our congregation or parish, denomination, or the universal church) values*. We often experience this aspect of an objective as an "ought" or "should" statement. It often emphasizes things people should know or be able to do if they are to participate fully in the ministry and mission of the church as the body of Christ. When we traveled to our parents' homes, for example, there were certain things we did and saw, people we met, and stories we told because we wanted our children to experience some of those things which have been important to our families. It was our judgment that these experiences were crucial as they claimed what it meant to be the heirs to the family heritage and to become the ancestors of the family's future.

Our curricular resources are one of the obvious places where we discover what our denomination or congregation values. In the unit I will be teaching, for example, the author tells us why it is important for us to begin a study of Peter. Through it, he suggests, we might identify with this intriguing, lively, and very human being whose life was transformed by his encounter with Christ. In the process we might begin to discover how God might transform our own lives.[2] In other words, we study Peter in part because he reveals how God works in and through people like ourselves.

This function of an objective prevents us from limiting our teaching to our own experience or to our pet ideas or concerns. It reminds us that as teachers we are agents of the heritage of the church. It is in our faithfulness to that heritage that we avoid the dangers of heresy and idolatry.

A third function of the objectives we use to guide our teaching is to connect our teaching to the interests, concerns, and needs of students. We have already discussed the diversity of interests, abilities, and needs in the persons we teach and the variation in values, experience, and cohesiveness from one group to the next. It is to the distinctive character of the persons we teach that this function of an objective is addressed. Our awareness of the lives of our students helps us to identify what they may need to continue on their faith journeys. Just as we needed to schedule stops to stretch our legs, to eat, to sleep, and to have a few moments to be by ourselves on our trip west, so those in our classes need certain information, experience, and skills to grow into responsible discipleship. In this case, an objective becomes concrete and local. It links the general concerns of the church to the specific realities of the people we teach. It makes the topics relevant to the circumstances and situations in which we teach. It is in our sensitivity to those we teach as we choose objectives that our teaching becomes relevant to them.

An objective also reveals the kind of educational experience we will be having. The objective in the resource we will be using on the life of Peter makes quite clear we will be engaged in study. We will be reading and discussing a printed resource. We will be analyzing biblical texts. The study will include reflective elements that are concerned with our spiritual growth—another educational experience. It will not be an educational experience emphasizing training, or mission, or involvement in a social action project. We will not be memorizing important information or texts. Neither will we be practicing in great detail behaviors considered crucial to the Christian life. Our emphasis will be upon study to open up new possibilities for understanding our faithfulness. When we are clear about the kind of educational experience we will be having, our teaching becomes more useful to those we teach.

If you would like to test the clarity of your objectives for teaching, complete the following section.

1. Write out an objective you used to guide a recent teaching plan or one you will be using in the near future. (It may be one stated in your curricular resources.)

2. What do you expect students to be able to do by the end of this session?

3. Are these expectations clear in your objective? If not, how would you restate the objective to make it clearer?

4. Why are these expectations important to the tasks of building up the body of Christ to glorify God and to serve neighbor?

5. What student interests and concerns will be addressed in a session guided by this objective?

6. What will students need to do to meet the expectations at work in this objective?

7. After reviewing questions 4, 5, and 6, how might you reword this objective to make clear to those you teach the expectations you have for this teaching-learning session?

CHAPTER 11

Content: The "What" of Teaching

With Christians through the centuries we declare that the life, death, and resurrection of Jesus Christ is the standard against which we measure the meaning and purpose of our lives. In the Christ we see a clue to the meaning of life both for that time two thousand years ago in Palestine and for our own time in the places where we live. We recognize in his teachings truth to guide our decisions and to direct our living. We see in his faithfulness to God's will an example for negotiating the tricky road between serving our self-interest and serving God.

In the Chirist we discern a clue to who we are. With the apostles we acknowledge—sometimes reluctantly, but sometimes wholeheartedly—that we are Christ's people. It is by that relationship we are known. It is through that relationship we are named. We are Christians. That relationship and name distinguishes us from our brothers and sisters around the world who find their identities in their relationships to Abraham and Moses, Buddha, Mohammed, or to some nation, value, or ideal.

It is through the Christ we also begin to understand whose we are. Even as Jesus Christ is known as the Son of God we begin to perceive what it means to be sons and daughters of God. We are the objects of God's love with all other peoples of the world. But as Christ's people we participate in God's creating and redeeming work. With Christ we find ourselves serving the vision of peace, love, and justice which we both seek and are charged to embody. In the historic language of the church, we become the hands, feet, and voice of the body of Christ wherever we may find ourselves.

The Christ event is the content of our teaching. We teach that people might know what it means to be Christ's people and what is expected of those who are Christ's people. The stories of the faith of the Hebrews and the early church, the doctrines, traditions, and liturgies of the centuries, and the lives of the saints all help us to understand the experience and the expectations of belonging to the community of faith we call Christian.

We teach that people might learn to see and to hear the world in the manner of Jesus Christ. I am reminded of the teacher, for example, who asked a group of junior high students to rewrite the parable of the good Samaritan as if it took place today. One student saw the Samaritan as a classmate who belonged to a group the families of that church considered socially unacceptable. Another saw the Samaritan as a union leader in the management headquarters of some large corporation. And one saw the Samaritan as a member of an ethnic minority discriminated against in that community while another saw the Samaritan as a communist. In all these examples, the students began to see the meaning of "neighbor" as Jesus saw it.

We also teach that people might develop the skills to assume the responsibilities of being agents of Christ in the world. The content of our teaching does not end with knowledge about our faith heritage or even with an awareness of what it may call us to do in our lives. It includes learning the skills crucial to act upon that awareness so that we in fact do glorify God and serve our neighbor.

We might say that our teaching is defined by the commandments to love God with all our heart, mind, soul, and strength and to love our neighbor as ourselves. To obey those commandments would reveal the extent of our identification with the Christ. The goal of our teaching would be total devotion to God. We would seek to align our teaching with the knowledge and will of God. We would, in other words, offer up our teaching as an expression of God's love for our neighbor.

As teachers we have a unique responsibility for the content of the Christ event. *We are to make that event and its meanings accessible to those we teach* with the expectation that they will make decisions regarding its importance to them. I have found Robert McAfee Brown's image of "opening up the past" to be helpful at this point. When we teach to "open up the past," we seek to identify and clarify what happened in the past. This part of our task is the most obvious. It deals with actual information we have about the life and ministry of Jesus as recorded by the early gospel writers. Sometimes it is couched in doctrinal and theological statements or "teachings" that have received the official approval of our denomination. As important as this information is, it is but a first step in opening up the Christ event to students. Unfortunately, too often teaching stops here. It is satisfied with the obvious or "literal" evidence in the event. It limits itself to a "lesson" about that event in the past. It reduces the event to a story, a formula, or a moral guideline for behavior.

The Christ event, however, stands in a continuum. It has its origins in creation and its fulfillment in the final establishment of the kingdom of God. The meanings of the Christ event only become accessible, consequently, when students begin to discover over the years the relationship between creation, covenant, and incarnation, of exodus and resurrection, of justice and salvation, and of history and eternity. The Christ event becomes accessible to students only as they begin to see its roots in the harmony of creation, the covenantal relationship between God and Israel, and the prophetic vision. The Christ event, in other words, becomes accessible insofar as students become increasingly familiar with it in all of its historical context. They begin to "know" it.

Similarly, the Christ event becomes important to those we teach when they begin to discover that it can make a difference in their own lives. They discover that possibility in the Scriptures in the stories of Peter, the several Marys, Martha, and Paul, whose encounters with the Christ transformed their lives. That same power becomes increasingly real to us as we see the influence of Christ through Augustine, St. Catherine of Siena, Martin Luther, and Dorothy Day, as well as through the lives of faithful people we know personally. It is through the stories of such people that we encounter the persistent relevance of the Christ event despite the radical social, political, and technological changes that occur in any age. The Christ event made a difference in the lives of women, men, and children in the early church. It continues to make a difference today. Its power is timeless.

For most of us the information and suggestions in the curricular resources we use provide the basis for our teaching. They set manageable boundaries on all that we could teach. They

69

provide an orderly sequence for engaging the Christ event in its historical context over the years. They identify what church officials and publishers believe is appropriate for an age group's encounter with that event. We may alter or expand that material to reflect our own experience and commitments, to use other knowledge and skills, or to be more responsive to the most pervasive issues or interests of those we teach. In spite of our reliance on these resources for determining the content of our teaching, however, we must still ask three questions regarding their adequacy. These questions reinforce those we asked of our objectives. Indeed, they reflect the mutuality of objective and content in our teaching.

1. *Is the content we plan to teach consistent with the heritage we have received?* In the Bible, the writers speak of the continuing vitality of the faith of Abraham and Moses for the present moment and into the future. The issue for us has to do with the extent to which we see our teaching as an extension of the faith of our ancestors. For most of us, our denominational relationships will mean that we view biblical history through the collective eyes of the Lutheran, Roman Catholic, Presbyterian, Baptist, Methodist, or Orthodox experience. But if we are truly faithful to the task of opening up the Christ event, we will begin to discover the interdependence of the faithfulness of all who call themselves after the name of Christ. This question is crucial because it prevents us from the dangers of heresy.

2. *Is the content of our teaching relevant to the pressing issues and circumstances of those we teach?* The Christ event is not an event confined to the past. It has its origin in the past, but it is a contemporary experience whenever and wherever it confronts people at the point of their basic values and commitments. The content of our teaching is not a relic of the past. It is the lively word of God addressed to people in fractured and abusive families, in schools more concerned with social control than with education, in jobs that value product more than worker, in government offices where responsibilities exceed the comprehension of everyone, in hospitals where the cost of new technology and basic health care often seem to clash, in nuclear disarmament talks, in places where people are hungry, and in the political prison camps of the world. These issues are as critical for children as for adults. All too many children know well the pain of fractured family life. They experience boredom and meaninglessness in much of their schooling. They fear the possibility of nuclear war. They are faced consistently with ethical and moral questions—often these questions are more complex than they can readily handle. This question is crucial because it has to do with the relevancy of our teaching in a world dominated by injustice, oppression, and the willful rejection of God's love for all people.

3. *Does the content of our teaching invite those we teach to seek to know more?* The Christ event cannot be confined to a rule, a doctrine, or a moral injunction. Indeed, the contrary is true. Whenever we successfully summarize the meanings of that event in a statement or two, we are surprised at the ways it bursts the bonds of our intentions and illuminates some new situation. Jesus, of course, illustrates this problem (or possibility) repeatedly. He not only obeyed the Hebrew law, for example, he transformed the law. He demonstrated that obedience is more than right action—it is right relationship. The attempt of teachers and curricular resources to summarize the meanings of the Christ event into a designated number of laws, commandments or guidelines for the life of faith

should be considered suspect. Most summaries are partial statements at best, but they lead people to think that they are the limits of the gospel. They stop growth in understanding and often of faith as well. This question is important because it prevents us from idolatrizing any part of the gospel and from limiting our students from growing beyond our own faithfulness.

Method: The "How" of Teaching

A method is simply the means we use to arrive at our destination.[3] When we travel we may choose to go by car or by air. For certain experiences our options increase. One can go by foot, by mule, or by boat into the Grand Canyon. To get about a large city we have to choose among subways, buses, taxis, trolleys, bicycles, and walking. The means of travel, the time we have available, and the cost all affect our decision. So does the kind of experience we seek. For example, if our destination is two thousand miles away and we make the trip to see important historical sights along the way, we would probably choose to travel by car rather than by airplane or train or perhaps even bus.

When we teach we are faced with similar choices. We have set an objective. We have a certain amount of time to reach that objective. The place, supplies, and the age, interest, and skills of the people whom we teach will also influence our selection of the means we will use to explore an issue or to experience an idea. So will our own experience with a given method. We are more likely to choose a way to engage students in a learning activity if we have experienced it ourselves and appreciate its possibilities. The danger, of course, is that we may choose a given method simply because we are familiar with it. We know what it requires of us in terms of preparation and we have had enough experience with it to anticipate how those we teach will respond to it. It may not be an appropriate method, however, to accomplish our objective for the session. Perhaps the most obvious illustration may be seen among teachers who feel most comfortable in the use of some "telling" method (lecture, storytelling, filmstrips, 16 mm film, etc.), yet who want their students to demonstrate their learning in concrete actions of faithfulness, morality, and neighborliness. "Telling" methods provide an excellent way to share information, to give an overview of an argument, to state or develop a point of view, but their potential for changing attitudes or behavior is rather low unless used with other methods.

In other words, after we have determined whether or not a method is appropriate for the age group, for the place we teach, for the time we have to teach, and if we can handle the cost of supplies and resources, we must still decide whether it will help us reach our objective. A method has several important characteristics which may clarify its usefulness for the task at hand.

In the first place, as Rudolf Bultmann has said, *a method is nothing more than a kind of questioning*. A method puts the question in motion. It activates our learning. It helps us begin to explore what we would like to know. But the method has a life of its own. If we wanted to see the major geysers in Yellowstone National Park and had only a morning to do so, we might best put ourselves on a tour bus and be led to each one. If we wanted to take pictures of the geysers for a photography exhibit, we would probably want to return several times unencumbered by tour guides, buses, and lots of fellow travelers. So we might choose to travel by car or bicycle.

A similar decision faces us in our teaching. We must be clear about the kind of question a particular method helps us to explore. For example, if we ask whether or not a method will help a student recall information at a later date or follow a set of instructions without having to think about them, we are evaluating its ability to help students memorize. We may then decide that the repetition of the desired behavior may be the most effective means to accomplish this goal. This is a common method used by drama teachers to help actors and actresses learn their lines, driving instructors to help people learn how to drive a car, and teachers in the church to help people learn some of the prayers and creeds used in worship.

As a process of asking questions, *a method invites students to try on, explore, and test the meaning and implication of a topic, issue, or task.* A method provides a structure for answering our questions. It poses a problem to be solved. It suggests a skill or attitude to be acquired. The method leads students out of the familiarity of what they already know, what they can already do, and how they feel about themselves or the topic or task at hand into an unknown territory. It can be an adventure. It can also be frightening. It can make us feel very vulnerable. This characteristic of a method is familiar to all of us. For example, when our family first went to Disneyland, our basic question was: "How can we have fun?" My wife and I tended to define "fun" as having a pleasant time. Our children expanded the meaning of the word to include a sense of excitement. In that technological theme park we had a choice of many "methods" or "rides" to engage us with our question. Some rides were pleasant. We knew exactly what we could expect from them. But for those of us who had never ridden a roller coaster, Space Mountain seemed awesome. It sounded exciting, but as we listened to the descriptions of others, some of us began to feel apprehensive. Yet for our children and later my wife (I still rejected that "thrill" from my definition of fun), the ride on Space Mountain was a high point in our quest (ion) for "fun." The same thing can happen in our teaching. The method structures our quest to understand, to sense, or to do something.

A method draws a student into the quest (ion). I am reminded of numerous junior high age students in several classes I have taught over the years who were asked to write contemporary paraphrases of given Bible passages as a part of their classroom experience. After reading the passage through several times and doing some background research they began to write. They did not finish within the time allotted, so they took their projects home. Their parents would tell me the students were so caught up in the task that they spent four, six and even eight hours on it. The method confronted them with something to do. It then asked what a biblical passage meant to them, caught their interest and imagination. Rather quickly they were drawn into the exercise. It took precedence over other interests and concerns. They suspended some of their other plans. They shifted their schedules. The method led them into an encounter with the Word of God.

It is at this point we discover one of the sources of resistance of people—especially teenagers and adults—to many methods. *Subconsciously people know that in any experience they may lose control of their own response to an event or situation.* Just as a child may be afraid of the unknown terrors of a dark room, many students resist a learning activity because they do not know what will be required of them.

I have known people who transferred from Bible study classes that used a method that led people to ask what they must do in their lives if they took the passage seriously to Bible classes

73

that used a method designed to explore the historical background of the Bible. I have known other people of all ages who avoided art methods because they feared they might reveal something about themselves they preferred to keep hidden. The method, in other words, often seems to have a life of its own. It engages us with the intent of our questions in very specific ways. Hearing a lecture about a parable of Jesus, doing a research project in the commentaries on that parable, painting a picture of the parable, or dramatizing the parable are each effective methods for exploring the meaning of the parable. But each will lead us to a different experience with the parable. Each may also lead us to different insights or responses through the parable.

A method also *creates a dialogue between students and the subject of their question.* This third characteristic of a method is illustrated in the way the tasks of research and paraphrase engaged the junior high students in a conversation between the biblical experience and their own. Perhaps one of the reasons I like to worship in congregations of black Christians in the United States is that the dialogical nature of the "method" of preaching is so evident. Both preacher and congregation enter into the question regarding what the Word of God has to say to us today. In most other settings such "lecture" methods also involve a dialogue, but the "listeners'" part is private and not seen as a public response.

The dialogue in either case is governed by the "rules" of the method. The more obvious rules are clarified by the instructions we give for a certain activity. If the method is a new one we may choose to demonstrate what is expected of the members of the class. If the method is finger painting, for example, the instructions or rules may include some of the following:

1. Put on a paint shirt.
2. Cover the table with newspapers.
3. Put the paints, water bucket, and sponges in the center of the table.
4. Sponge the paper given to you for your picture with water. Don't let it get too wet.
5. Choose the colors you wish to use and start painting.
6. When you finish, hang the painting up.
7. Clean up your place, wash your hands.
8. Help put up the paint supplies.

These rather obvious instructions reveal one set of rules. Another set is implicit. They have to do with the materials used in the method. These rules shape the dialogue between the student and the subject of his or her question. It is in the interaction of the student with the paint that these rules become self-evident. They have to do with getting your fingers in the paint, with the amount of pressure used in applying the paint to the paper, the kinds of motions one uses to convey certain thoughts or feelings prompted by the question, the consequences of running a red line through a blue line, and so forth. The rules of the method, in other words, create a dialogue between the painter and the possibilities of the method to give expression to the student's quest (ion).

This illustration leads us to a fourth characteristic of a method. *A method makes a demand of those who use it.* This same point may be made another way. A method has the potential to reveal new possibilities for us. If we are going to finger-paint, or lecture, or conduct a discussion, we must come to terms with what is being asked of those we teach. For example, after a few strokes with the finger paints we soon discover that if we want any kind of design we must learn how to integrate our paint strokes, our choice of color, and our mental image of the product we want to create. As we allow these issues to dominate our attention, we begin to settle down. We start to make deliberate decisions about which color and what stroke to make.

We begin to concentrate on the task. We may make a mistake. We may throw that effort away. We try another. Perhaps we try still another. We may lose all sense of time and place in the intensity of our concentration. The same thing can happen with any method. Remember those discussions that became so intense your class sessions ran overtime? Remember the awesome quietness that followed a role play or the telling of a story? Remember the explosions of ideas and questions that followed some lectures?

It is in the potential of the method to demand something of us that the resistance of students is intensified. Their caution, revealed in their resistance, should be taken seriously. When we as teachers introduce a given method as a way of engaging students in a question, we have no control over the outcome of that decision. If the method truly invites persons to take seriously the question, and engages them in dialogue, we rarely know how they will respond to the demands it places on them.

I am reminded of a woman in a teacher-training event who participated with all of us in finger-painting our images of God. This activity had been designed to give teachers of young people an experience with a method many had never used. The leadership training objective was to develop familiarity with the method. The method was to be used later with a group of seventh and eighth graders. In that session, it was to become the means for the students to explore their images of God. But for this young woman, these objectives were transposed. As she entered into the activity, the dialogue between her feelings and the colors became increasingly tense. Her picture became darker and darker until it was a black and purple mass of jumbled lines. In a tiny corner of the page was one yellow spot. This harmless method (or so we thought) became the occasion for her to face the anger she felt toward a God who would allow her husband to leave her. The method, moreover, revealed her deepest and, up to this point, well-hidden feelings to everyone present. She was suddenly vulnerable in a way she had never expected to be. She was also free in a way she did not know was possible. The method had become a channel to encounter the grace of God in the midst of that teaching event. But that is a risk a lot of people do not wish to take. It is also a risk a lot of us who teach are afraid to have happen through our teaching. We want people to learn and to grow. But we rarely like to face up to what that process of transformation may exact from either those we teach or ourselves.

The danger is that we as teachers and our students will choose methods that rarely make demands on us. Teachers who insist that activities be fun for children and teens often fall into this category. Students who prefer discussion to any other method have often learned how to keep a conversation on safe grounds. They have learned the method well enough; they can prevent it from engaging them. For example, adult Bible classes that limit their discussions to what is obviously in the Bible have learned how to keep the Word of God away from the pains and joys of their daily lives. Once in a while, the situation or a student's persistence in pursuing a question will reveal once again the power of the method to engage us with an issue, idea, or task. That moment may intensify fear in those we teach or it might become the occasion for a renewed openness to the transforming power of God. It is as we face up to the demand of a method on the lives of both teachers and students that the quality of the care in a class becomes crucial. If people believe that others will listen with sensitivity and empathy; if they know that others will reach out to them when they are vulnerable; if they know that others will also be taking risks from time to time—they will be much more open to the possibilities in a given method to engage them with the subject of their deepest question. A teaching-learning community whose care reveals the gracefulness of God also reveals the encouragement of God to grow in grace, in wisdom, and in truth.

The question, of course, in planning a teaching-learning event has to do with what method to choose. This task is related to what we want the method to accomplish. In the chart that follows is listed a series of questions that guide our expectations of any teaching-learning event. In the second column is a list of methods that can be used to realize these questions. It should be noted that a method may be used for all questions after the one with which it is listed. For example, a lecture or a slide presentation can be used with each question. The reverse is also true. A method will not fulfill our expectations for any question listed before it. For example, parable writing is not an effective method for memorizing information.

One other word needs to be said about the appropriateness of a method for people of different ages. It is my contention that any method can be used with any age group. It is not the method in and of itself that makes the difference. It is how we use it. It is obvious that we may share an idea with some two-year-olds for two to three minutes. For young adults we might expand an idea into a forty-five minute lecture. The method is the same; it has been adapted to the skills and abilities of the age group. Consequently, one of the issues critical for teachers after choosing a method is to ensure that its use is appropriate to the age group.

For those who would like to know—

1. *What methods will help*
   students
       retain information,
       attitudes, or skills?

   Repetition
   Recitation
   Behavior modification (methods that
       reward desired behavior, punish
       undesired behavior)
   Drill
   Memory games and exercises
   Directed reading
   Testing (fill-in the blanks,
       incomplete sentences, quiz
       games, etc.)
   Audiovisuals
   Guided research activities
   Flash cards
   Imitation

___

2. What methods will help students
   demonstrate what they know and what
   they can do?

   All of the above plus
   Making maps or charts
   Writing reports
   Photography
   Following guided instructions
       for an exercise or task
   Trial-and-error problem-solving
       exercises
   Directed performance activities
       (music, drama, games, sports,
       worship)

___

3. What methods help students
   interpret what they know?
   These methods help to explore
   the meaning of a learning task.

   All of the above plus
   Creative writing
   Creative arts (murals, posters,
       drawings, etc.)
   Creative dramatics (including
       puppets, role play, skits,
       mime)
   Exercises involving the use of the
       imagination and fantasy
   Creative play

4. What methods help students demonstrate that they can use their knowledge and skills in solving life-like problems? In other words, what methods help students apply what they know?

All of the above plus
Discussion
Experimental activities in which students test a hypothesis
Problem-solving activities
Apprenticeships in which students work under the supervision of a "master" teacher on some task or project

---

5. What methods help students analyze an issue or problem with the intention of clarifying it?

All of the above plus
Research
Case studies
Graphs
Charts
Multiple choice tests
Computer programs
Simulation games
Exegesis (a method for analyzing literary texts—especially in the Bible)

---

6. What methods help students solve problems requiring original and creative thought? In other words, what methods help students to synthesize what they know in the creation of something new?

All of the above plus
Creating designs for a project or activity
Developing hypotheses and theories
Creating a plan for a class, activity, or program
Activities that call for interpretations of an idea or action

---

7. What methods help students decide what is appropriate, right, good, or true?

Activities that explore options with the expectation that people will make decisions (e.g., values clarification exercises)

For those who would like to explore the appropriateness of a given method for a teaching activity, use the following questions.

1. What is the method?

2. What does it require people to do?

3. Does this method have the potential to ask students to engage in the learning task you want them to do—e.g., to retain information, to demonstrate knowledge or skills, etc.? See chart above. yes _____ no _____

4. What instructions would the age group you teach need in order to use this method?

5. As you look over those instructions, can you think of persons who might have difficulty because of physical or mental abilities? yes _____ no _____ If so, who? _____
   _____

6. Can the method be adapted to include these persons more fully? If so, in what ways?

7. How long will it take to use this method in your teaching session?

8. Is there enough time to use it? yes _____ no _____

9. Can the method be used effectively in the place you teach? yes _____ no _____

10. Does the method reflect a sensitivity to cultural patterns of learning? If not, in what ways might the method be adapted to account for these cultural factors?_____

   _____
   _____
   _____
   _____
   _____

11. What supplies and materials are needed?

	Are they available?	If not, can they be obtained?	If not, can substitutions be found?

For those who would like to explore how to use some of the methods listed in this chapter, the following books provide guidelines and suggestions.

Dotts, M. Franklin and Maryann. *Clues to Creativity: Providing Learning Experiences for Children*. New York: Friendship Press, 1974, 1975, 1976. Three volumes.

This extensive survey of methods that may be used in teaching is arranged alphabetically through three volumes. The authors describe the methods and tell where, why, and how to use them. The supplies needed are listed. An extensive bibliography of other method resources is found at the conclusion of the third volume. Although the books are directed toward those working with children, they are useful for teachers and leaders of teen and adult classes as well.

Gangel, Kenneth. *24 Ways to Improve Your Teaching*. Wheaton, Ill.: Victor Books, 1982 (1974).

The author discusses what each method on an extensive list of methods can do in fulfilling the goals of a teacher. Helpful guidance is given for everything from lecture to field trips, memorization, and creative writing.

Griggs, Donald L. *20 New Ways of Teaching the Bible*. Nashville: Abingdon Press, 1979.

The title identifies the content of this book. The suggested approaches to teaching the Bible have the potential to enliven Bible study for older children, teens, and adults.

Griggs, Patricia. *Creative Activities in Church Education*. Nashville: Abingdon Press, 1980.

This guide to the use of dramatic, musical, visual, and writing methods to evoke the creativity in learners is especially helpful to the teacher who does not feel creative but would like to have a classroom that is. The author provides clear instructions for setting up, doing, and exploring the meanings of a creative activity.

Layman, James E. *Using Case Studies in Christian Education*. Scottsdale, Ariz: National Teacher Education Project, 1977.

This book provides guidelines for using case studies in the teaching of older children, teens, or adults, as well as suggestions for teachers and leaders who would like to write cases for use in the classroom.

⚑

Strategy: The "When and Where" of Teaching

Finally! All of the discussion we have had so far leads us to the crucial step of creating a strategy for teaching a specific session. A strategy for teaching functions much like an itinerary for the traveler. We take it with us. It is a road map telling us our starting point and destination with all the stops in between. It identifies things to see and do along the way. It gives an estimate of how much time it takes to travel from one stop to the next. It may well list special equipment and supplies or provide pertinent information so that we may be ready for whatever we may encounter.

For volunteer teachers a strategy is a plan of action for our teaching. It identifies our starting place. It describes how we may get everyone "on board," so that all who participate may enter fully into our plans. It also identifies our destination—what it is that our students are supposed to experience or do during the session. And it outlines each of the activities that lead the members of the class toward that destination.

The elements in a plan of action for teaching are essentially the same whether we are teaching children, teenagers, or adults. A survey of curricular resources will demonstrate the similarity of format in the plans for teaching persons of any age. The reasons may be obvious. Every plan has an objective. Every plan is a design to convey some information, or value, or skill. Every plan creates a sequence or strategy for activities to engage students with the content and experience of teaching.

There are differences in the amount of responsibility volunteer teachers assume in developing that plan of action. These differences will be based on the extent to which a teacher decides

1. what *should* be taught in a session or series from all that *could* be taught from the heritage and mission of the church.

2. what is appropriate to teach a specific group of people given their stages of physical, intellectual, moral, and faith development and their particular historical and cultural situation.

3. what methods will most effectively engage students in learning experiences.

These differences are evident in three approaches I have seen teachers use when developing a plan of action for teaching. All three work. Each has strengths and each has problems. The one you or I choose to follow will be based upon such things as

1. the extent of our knowledge of the content we teach and our experience in teaching.

2. the time we have available to plan.

3. the expectations of our congregation, parish, or denomination regarding what shall be taught.

4. the emphasis we place upon being original in developing a teaching plan.

Our decision regarding which of the three approaches to take will be based upon our evaluation of each of these concerns. In actual practice, we may well use all three approaches over an extended period of time or in different situations. But most of us will tend to follow one approach more than the other two.

Planning Strategy #1

In this approach, a plan of action for teaching is prescribed. It is either a part of a denominational curriculum plan or a part of a curricular resource purchased from a religious publisher or previously developed by a congregational committee. The role of the teacher is to become so familiar with the plan that it becomes his or hers. It may involve deciding which of several optional activities to use in a teaching session. It clearly requires the teacher to gather the necessary resources, to set up the place for teaching, and to become familiar with the content to be communicated and the methods to be used.

Because most volunteer teachers use resources approved by their denomination or prepared by religious publishing houses, this approach to planning is probably the most commonly used. It has numerous strengths as an approach to planning. It makes an efficient use of a teacher's time—a major concern of religious educators early in this century. It is a part of a larger curricular design. Previous units of study lead into the one you or I might use, just as it lays the groundwork for further study. Because people across a denomination may be using the same resource, it provides a common experience in the denomination for building a common language and experience for its people.

There are problems to this approach, however. Teachers often act as if they were uninvolved in the content of their own teaching. The teacher is the agent of the writer's religious experience and understandings. Because these plans of action for teachers were prepared for hundreds of teachers, moreover, they may not reflect the special gifts or the particular needs of either teachers or students. And yet, in spite of such problems, many people in the church have encountered the gospel through teaching guided by this first approach to planning.

Planning Strategy #2

A second approach to planning is an adaptation of the first. In this case a teacher works within the basic framework of the plan suggested by the author of a given curricular resource. Two things, however, may lead the teacher to introduce new and different content, an alternative method into the plan of action, or a revised sequence of learning experiences. The teacher may decide that the content of the resource does not address some of the questions, concerns, or needs of class members. In other words, the specific agenda of this group of people is not met by the author's attempt to develop a plan for a wide diversity of teaching situations.

The teacher may also decide that a method suggested by the resource will not work. The reasons may vary for this decision. Sometimes we reject a given method because we are unfamiliar with it, or because the group has had a bad experience using it, or because we do not have the resources or space to use it. We may decide, based on our previous experience, that it is less effective than another method to engage students with the content of our teaching. We may also decide that the method is not as appropriate to the developmental skills or cultural values or heritage of the particular group we teach as one we might choose. Our reasons might be legitimate or not. In a sense that is not the issue, unless the alternative method we choose makes it possible for both students and us to ignore or avoid the claim of the content of our teaching on our lives.

In my own teaching in the church I probably use this approach the most. It allows me to work within the framework developed by those responsible for curriculum resources in my denomination and at the same time to be responsive to the uniqueness of the class I teach. It provides more opportunity for the creative efforts of a teacher without placing unrealistic demands upon a teacher's time.

Although this approach may seem ideal, it also has several problems. It opens the door to a teacher to reject anything in a curriculum plan with which he or she may disagree. It can lead to an overemphasis on a teacher's major concerns or values to the exclusion of others cherished by the church through the ages. In other words, the use of this approach can be the means by which teachers avoid encountering the content developed in a curricular resource for their own lives. It may also have been chosen as a way to avoid the disciplines of teaching outlined in the curricular resource. And yet, many people have been challenged to be faithful disciples by teachers who have used this approach to planning for their teaching.

Planning Strategy #3

A third approach to creating a plan of action for teaching requires the most creativity on the part of the teacher. In this approach teachers originate every step in the plan of action. Drawing upon all the resources available to them, they attempt to fashion a unit of study into a series of sessions that reflect both the commitments and skills of the teacher and the interests and needs of the students in the light of the theological and faith commitments of the congregation or parish and its denomination. This approach, if done well, obviously takes the most time, but it also tends to heighten the excitement and investment of the teacher. It engages students at the point of the teacher's own encounter with the gospel. In this case, the plan can be a very personal expression of the teacher's involvement with the topics and issues being explored. This approach, if not taken seriously by the teacher, however, all too often ends up as a superficial experience for students. It can trivialize the gospel into whatever happens to catch a teacher's or a group's fancy. It can be undisciplined and disjointed, providing little sense of the relationship of one learning experience to another. For example, I know of young adults who never explored the Old Testament in their church education experience because their teachers used this approach. The greatest danger in this approach is the fragmentation it can create in a student's religious education experience. Yet, when it is part of an overall design in a congregation or parish and is done well, it too has led many people into a life of faithful discipleship.

A plan of action, or strategy, clarifies the purpose and direction of our teaching. It also makes visible our understanding of our role as mediators of God's grace. It reveals something of the content of our own commitments and gives expression to our calling to teach. Moreover, it is a sign of our preparation and readiness for the task at hand—to engage in the teaching act.

EXAMPLE

1. The objective or theme for the overall unit or series:

2. The objective(s) for this session:

	Projected time activity needs	Who is responsible?	Supplies needed

3. What will class members do as they arrive?   _____ _____ _____
   _____ _____ _____

   What instructions will they need?   _____

4. How will you introduce the session—its objectives and activities?   _____

5. What is the next step or activity in your plan?   _____

   What instructions will they need?   _____

The Ministry of the Volunteer Teacher

For those who would like to improve their planning, study the following suggestions and adapt them to your own situation.

1. Request two sets of curricular resources from the person who orders them for your congregation or parish. One set is to be used for reading and reference. The second is to be cut up and used in the development of your own teaching plan.

2. Purchase a three-ring notebook, or file folder, and paper. You will also need pen, scissors, and cellophane tape or glue.

3. Follow an outline for a teaching strategy such as the one given above.
   a. Cut and paste the objective statement from the curricular resource into your notebook.
   b. Then move through the teaching plan cutting out those instructions, stories, and interpretations of the subject matter you are exploring and intend to use in your teaching.
   c. Write out or add other material you have decided to substitute for material in the curricular resource.

When you have finished, the material in the notebook is your own plan for teaching. It omits all the extra material included in the curricular resource and it adds those parts which best reflect your own knowledge, skill, and commitments. You will also have a good record of your plans for future reference.

CHAPTER 14

Evaluation: The "What Happened" While Teaching

The first creation story in Genesis 1 concludes with the familiar words: "God looked at everything he had made, and he was very pleased." (Gen. 1:31a TEV) The attitude attributed to God is a familiar one in our own experience. We finish a project, look it over, and declare it to be "good." We describe a recent vacation or outing to a friend and conclude that "we had a tremendous time." We stop in the midst of a teaching session, recall the flow of the session, the high level of involvement of the students, and acknowledge to ourselves that it is an "exciting" session. In each instance, we are involved in the process of evaluation. We review the information we have, and we assess it against some standard or criteria.

We use evaluation for a variety of purposes. In the illustrations above, evaluation becomes the occasion for *celebration*. It is the basis for affirming both the quality and the product of our effort. It is the source of the pleasure that often prompts us to move into the future with confidence and hope.

The biblical record illustrates other uses for evaluation. In another familiar passage we find the prophet Nathan confronting King David with the disparity between his values and his actions (II Samuel 12:1-15). In recounting the incident Robert McAfee Brown has observed that David apparently did not realize he was guilty of adultery, deception, and murder. Perhaps he believed that he was simply exercising a little kingly prerogative in his seduction of Bathsheba; as commander-in-chief he certainly could send any of his soldiers where he wanted them to go. His actions, however, did not go unnoticed. Nathan, hearing the ensuing "palace scuttlebutt," accepted, although undoubtedly with reluctance, the responsibility of helping David to face up to the meaning of his actions and to accept the consequences of them. His method was a simple one. He told a story of a rich man with great flocks stealing the one ewe lamb of a very poor man to butcher and serve to his guests. David, who is caught up in the story, completely misses the similarity between the story and his own recent behavior. He is outraged and condemns the selfish act of the rich man. Nathan then points out the obvious, and David is filled with remorse and penitence.[4] Nathan used a rather creative process to help David evaluate his own behavior. That is a helpful clue to the variety of ways one can engage in evaluation. For our purposes, however, this story illustrates the importance of evaluation as a basis for *confession*. It helps us to face up to the conflict between our ideals and our actions, our calling and our response, as well as the disparity between what we say we will do and what we actually do.

Jesus repeatedly illustrated a third use of evaluation. In a variety of ways he presented his listeners with evidence calling for a *decision* that could radically alter their lives in the future. His encounter with a rich man illustrates the process. This man, obviously wealthy by his dress and apparently in the way he carried himself, comes to Jesus and asks what he must do to inherit eternal life. Jesus recounts what is expected of the faithful Jew—to obey the commandments. But this the man had done religiously since he was young, and the effort apparently still left him with a sense of incompleteness. Jesus, of course, was a perceptive person. He quickly observed the source of the man's dissatisfaction and said, "You need only one thing. Go and sell all you have and give the money to the poor." (Mark 10:21a TEV) The decision was the rich man's. He examined the alternatives. In this instance, evaluation clarifies options. It may suggest the appropriate choice for us and our situation. Just as in the case of the rich man, however, the decision is ours.

Evaluation is an important ongoing process in every aspect of our lives. Perhaps we pay so little attention to it simply because it is a process. Our attention is drawn instead to its consequences. Three I have mentioned. Evaluation provides the data which allows us to celebrate our victories, accomplishments, and breakthroughs. It also forces us to acknowledge our failures, misguided adventures, and outright sinfulness. And it helps us to clarify the decisions we must make to shape our futures. These three experiences are crucial to the life of any group and especially to any group participating in the task of building up the body of Christ.

Appropriate celebration renews and energizes a group. It intensifies a sense of common bond and purpose. It provides momentum from the present into the future. It reminds one of the source of the enriching experiences of life. Apathy, even despair, are the experiences of groups that do not experience the revitalizing power of celebration.

Confession cleanses the life of a group. It rids a group of the hold of forces on its perceptions and actions that hamper its work, create divisions among its members, or blind it to its purposes and primary loyalties. Confession frees us from burdening the future of a group with the problems of its past. It makes possible a sense of new beginnings in the midst of reconciled relationships and renewed purposes.

A group makes decisions if it believes it has a future. When a group clarifies alternatives and sets a course of action, it moves beyond the status quo and the pattern of "we've always done it this way." Ultimately, the ability to decide is crucial if a group is to respond faithfully to God's call in whatever new situation it may find itself.

We may experience celebration, confession, and moments of decision in highly personal ways. Yet in the teaching-learning situation these acts are often public events. They are based on an evaluative process involving all participants. Unfortunately, we tend to leave the evaluative process up to individuals after the session or class is completed. Evaluation that occurs in hallways, over the phone, or in a casual conversation between two people rarely affects the life and work of the total group or class in constructive or creative ways. These observations lead me to identify several principles to guide our efforts to evaluate our teaching.

1. Evaluation is more effective if all members of a class or group participate in the process.
2. Evaluation is more effective if all persons contribute relevant information to the evaluative process.
3. Evaluation is more effective if the information given is checked for accuracy before it is accepted and used.

4. Evaluation is more effective if the standards for assessing the information or experience are clear to everyone.
5. Evaluation is more effective if it is used in some way to improve the quality of the teaching-learning experience.
6. Evaluation is more effective if the method(s) used to gather and assess the information or experience is related to the goals or objectives of the evaluation exercise. (See chapter 12 for selecting appropriate methods for evaluation as well as teaching.)
7. Evaluation is more effective in the teaching ministry if the primary point of reference is always the gracious activity of God as the source and end of all our teaching effort.

Evaluation is often seen as the final act in a meeting or program. Actually it is the occasion for the revitalization of an activity or program in process and for the development of new possibilities and directions. It clarifies the extent of the faithfulness of our teaching plan to the values and heritage we have received, and it helps to reveal what we have to do to prepare ourselves for our teaching tasks in the future. In the process it may help us refine our gifts for teaching even as we engage in teaching others. It may further enrich our understanding of our call to teach, and it may deepen our commitment to the fulfillment of that call.

Evaluation should be one of the most creative moments in our teaching. Rarely have I experienced it that way. Evaluation is too often judgmental or trivial. In either case, the information it gathers is not usable. It does not lead us to celebration, confession, or decision. When it works, however, evaluation can be powerful. It was during the formal evaluations of a teacher-training event I participated in as I started seminary that I began to see myself as a Christian educator. It was during the evaluation of an adult class that a group of people decided to engage in a mission activity in the community. I have seen children and teenagers reestablish broken relationships during evaluative moments in their classes. I have also heard people clarify their commitments to serve as disciples of Jesus Christ during times of evaluation. Such moments are full of grace. They are filled with the energizing power of the Holy Spirit. They became occasions for facing the future with a sense of purpose and hope. In those instances evaluation effectively increased the power of the teaching in those classes.

For those who would like to identify ways of gathering information that is basic to any useful evaluation process:

There are several ways of gathering information about what students do while you teach, for clues regarding what students are learning, and for evidence of your own teaching effectiveness.

Observation (Effective with all age groups)

1. The most obvious way to gather information is to recall what you have seen and heard. This information can be checked with members of the class or other teachers in the room for accuracy.

2. Many teachers ask an outsider to observe a session to gather information for evaluation. This information is most useful if it has been written down using the process of observation. Often this person is in a supervisory role: superintendent, coordinator, or pastor.

Feedback (We can obtain information about what happened from children as young as four or five. They usually report, however, only what they did rather than what they felt or learned.) There are many ways to obtain information from people about their experience.

1. Direct questions by the teacher or leader may gather information either verbally or through some written form. The form of the question will determine whether the information you receive is to be based on feelings or what people actually said or did.

2. Questionnaires—often in the form of a checklist—provide a quick way of identifying a range of perceptions of an activity.

3. Open-ended sentences identify the subject and leave the conclusion to those providing the information. (E.g., The most interesting part of today's session was _____.) These responses can be either verbal or written. I have even seen them put to music.

4. Images of feelings and reactions often through the use of art media, but also through music, provide a subjective but often profound source of information about an event or experience.

Testing provides evidence of the ability to recall and make use of learning. It reveals information regarding the way students are able to make connections between knowledge and skills, their retention of information, and their ability to use the experience from a teaching session in new and original ways. Much testing can be done in groups—e.g., games, creative projects, problem-solving exercises, simulation games, and demonstration activities.

Postscript

t is Easter Sunday afternoon as I write these words. We have just returned from the celebration of the resurrection of Christ. The trumpets dramatized the exhilaration we felt as we sang "Christ the Lord Is Risen Today." The anthems and preaching proclaimed the joy of the day. It was a good Easter service.

The depth of the power of that event, however, is due in part to the familiarity we bring to hearing the Easter story once again. Its significance occurs as our hearing reveals new meaning and new hope through those familiar words. Our hearing and responding to this most holy of days in the Christian year may be traced in part, to the commitment of teachers through the centuries to tell and retell that story and to explain and reinterpret its meanings for the challenges and decisions that face each new generation. Teachers often lack the visibility of other leaders in the church, but their contribution to the building up of the church to glorify God and to serve our neighbors is a crucial one.

As we conclude our conversation, we celebrate the work of the volunteer teacher. We are grateful for your teaching. In the words of J. Stanley Glen, your work is the "fleshly spear-head of the gospel." You bring its meaning to bear on the worlds of children, teenagers, and adults in the communities in which you live. Your faithfulness to handing on the traditions of faith cuts through the claim of other gods on their lives. Your openness to God's call to love and justice prompts those you teach to entertain the visions of peace and righteousness that also enlivened the faith of Moses, Isaiah, and Paul.

We may not often experience such power when we encounter a lively group of children, a questioning group of teens, or a group of adults who seem to resist any probing discussion during any given class session. Over a period of time we do catch glimpses of the learnings of our students and we may chance on some change in their attitudes or behaviors that indicates an increasing openness to the leading of the Holy Spirit in their lives. We may even have the opportunity to explore with a student now and then a major decision of faith. But it may be during an Easter service that we begin to discover the effect of our teaching: in the open attentiveness to the hope envisioned in that event; as we hear children joining in the prayers and hymns; as we watch teenagers expectantly receiving the bread and wine; as those of any age comment later on the relationship of something in the sermon to something discussed in class. It is in the knowing expectation, however, of a congregation united in the worship of God that we may begin to witness fully the effects of our teaching.

The Ministry of the Volunteer Teacher

In a similar fashion we may begin to see the accumulative effects of the teaching in a congregation or parish during a committee meeting in which the options to a decision are examined for their effectiveness in witnessing to the grace of God. Perhaps it becomes evident whenever we observe the open response of people to the concrete needs of those around them or when a decision made by someone reveals a sensitivity to the ethical implications involved in discipleship to Jesus Christ. The ultimate reward for our efforts, in other words, is not to be found in the classroom, as important as that may be, but in the quality and the faithfulness of the worship and service of our congregations and parishes.

On this Easter, I have been reminded of the ministry of the teachers of the church, who through the ages and throughout the world continue to tell the stories of Jesus and of God's redemptive love. We have been graced by their faithfulness to the task. We are also graced by your commitment to the task. Thanks be to God!

Easter, 1985

NOTES

Notes for Part I

1. For an extended discussion of this view of community, see Charles R. Foster, *Teaching in the Community of Faith* (Nashville: Abingdon Press, 1982), chap. 1.
2. Walter Brueggemann, *The Creative Word: Canon as a Model for Biblical Education* (Philadelphia: Fortress Press, 1982), p. 1.
3. James B. Dunning, *Ministries: Sharing God's Gifts* (Winona, Minn.: St. Mary's Press, 1980), p. 15.

Notes for Part II

1. Brueggemann, p. 1.
2. *Ibid.*, p. 20.
3. *Ibid.*, p. 16.
4. *Ibid.*, p. 15.
5. For an extended discussion of the communal character of our personal identities, see Foster, *Teaching in the Community of Faith*, chaps. 1 and 2; John H. Westerhoff III, *Building God's People in a Materialistic Society*, (New York: The Seabury Press, 1983); Brueggemann, chap. 2; and Mary Elizabeth Moore, *Education for Continuity and Change: A New Model for Christian Religious Education* (Nashville: Abingdon Press, 1983), chaps. 3 and 5.

Notes for Part III

1. A statement by Patrick Swazos Hinds, Tesque Pueblo artist, posted in the Pueblo Cultural Center, Albuquerque, New Mexico, October, 1978.

Notes for Part IV

1. I am using the word *objective* to describe that which serves as the destination or end of our efforts. Many people use the word *goal* to mean the same thing.
2. Joseph S. Wang, *Peter* (Nashville: Graded Press, 1980), p. 6.
3. I am indebted to my graduate assistant, David Otto, whose research and analysis of the function of method in religious education has been an invaluable aid to the development of this chapter.
4. Robert McAfee Brown, *Unexpected News: Reading the Bible with Third World Eyes* (Philadelphia: Westminster Press, 1984), p. 55.

FOR FURTHER READING
ON THE MINISTRY OF TEACHING

Bowman, Locke E. Jr. *Teaching Today: The Church's First Ministry*. Philadelphia: Westminster Press, 1980; especially the section on "Teaching/Process of Activitating."

Foster, Charles R. *Teaching in the Community of Faith*. Nashville: Abingdon Press, 1982; especially chapter 4, "Teaching: a Responsibility of the Community of Faith."

Groome, Thomas H. *Christian Religious Education: Sharing Our Story and Vision*. San Francisco: Harper and Row, 1980; especially part 6, "The Copartners in Christian Religious Education."

Little, Sara. *To Set One's Heart: Belief and Teaching in the Church*. Atlanta: John Knox Press, 1983.

Nouwen, Henri J. *Creative Ministry: Beyond Professionalism in Teaching, Preaching, Counseling, Organizing, and Celebrating*. Garden City: Doubleday, 1978; especially chapter 1, "Beyond the Transference of Knowledge: Teaching."

Wingeier, Douglas E. *Seven Biblical Images of Teaching*. Nashville: Discipleship Resources (of The United Methodist Church).

DATE DUE

FEB 10 '94			
JUL 24 1996			

DEMCO 38-297